The Operation and Management of a Software Company

I0394319

An Entrepreneurial Guide to Creating and Maintaining a Software Development Company

Written By
Larry G. Miner

Edited By
Argie Miner and Lia Fresty

Copyright 2004 by Larry Miner, 2004 by Larry Miner
Illustrations copyright 2004 by Larry Miner
ISBN: 1-4392-3905-3
ISBN-13: 9781439239056

The Operation and Management of a Software Company.
An Entrepreneurial Guide to Creating and Maintaining a Software Development Company

All rights reserved. No part of this publication may be reproduced, stored in a retrieval system, or transmitted, in any form or by any means, electronic, mechanical, photocopying, recording, or otherwise, without the prior written permission of the publisher.

Printed in the United States

Published By

Larry Miner
PO Box 587
Bath, Ohio 44210

To My Editors

Argie - *omnia vincit amor*

Gravitation is not responsible for people falling in love.
   —Albert Einstein

Lia - *verbatim et litteratim*

I just thought of something funny...your mother.
   —Cheech Marin

Thank you so much for *All* your patience.

Contents

Chapter 1   Introduction   1

    What is this book about?
    To whom does the book speak?
    What this book is not
    A workbook
    My perspective
    A final note

Chapter 2   How to use this Book   3

    Where to start reading
    Diagram – Business Workflow

Chapter 3   The Staff   7

    Introduction
    Personality of the Owner
    Think about it
    A common mistake
    Personality of the team
    Locate, interview, hire and build a
          development staff
    How the three skill sets work together
    The structure of a development environment
    Get the most from your staff
    Managing a Development Workforce
    Form – Example Employment Contract

Chapter 4   The Staff Structure   53

    Introduction
    Sales People
    Project Managers
    Technical Writer

A Technical Writer's Job
　　　The Developer
　　　The Project Manager & Technical Writer as part of
　　　　　the Sales Department
　　　Diagram – Staff Structure

Chapter 5   The Cost of Development　　　　　　61

　　　Introduction
　　　Cost of Employees
　　　Cost of Internal Operations
　　　Overhead Costs
　　　Billable Hours - costs of not controlling them
　　　What are efficiency rates?
　　　Development
　　　Internal Project Tracking
　　　Internal Productivity
　　　Form – Daily Time Sheet
　　　Form – Training Repayment Agreement

Chapter 6   The Cost of Management &　　　　　83
　　　　　　　Administration

　　　Efficiency of In-house Staff
　　　Project Managers
　　　Accounting / Administration
　　　Clerical / Administration Management
　　　Other Costs to Consider and Control

Chapter 7   The Design Specification　　　　　　95

　　　Introduction
　　　Re-Engineering
　　　A New Software Application
　　　Writing the Specification
　　　The Customer
　　　Your Business' Use

Structure of the Design Document
Table of Contents
A Example of a Simpler Table of contents
A Example of a Complex Table of contents
The Purpose of a Design Specification

Chapter 8   Estimating the Design Specification   117

Introduction
Connection
Tools to Use
A Simple Estimating Spreadsheet
Review of the spreadsheet
A second type of spreadsheet
Pros and Cons
The Completed Estimate
Example – Simple Spreadsheet
Example – Complex Spreadsheet

Chapter 9   Developing the Application   125

Introduction
By this Time
The Project Manger
The Developers
The Technical Writer
The Customer
Accounting
Keeping on Track
The Bottom Line

Chapter 10   The Project Book   131

The Project Book
Birth – The Sales Department
Life – The Project Manager
Retirement – The Sales Department

Chapter 11   Change and Issue Orders   137

    Introduction
    Change Orders
    Issue Orders
    Form – Change Order
    Form – Issue Order

Chapter 12   Daily Developer Notes   143

    Daily Developer Notes

Chapter 13   Invoicing for Services Rendered   145

    Invoicing
    Terms
    Spreadsheet Line Items
    Sending It
    Prior to the Due Date
    Faxing
    Collecting
    Other Accounting

Chapter 14   Revenues and the Contract   149

    Introduction
    Charging for Services Rendered
    Methods of Charging
    Time and Materials
    A Fixed Bid
    The Lynch Pin
    A Contract that works for both parties
    Tracking Time
    The Company Lawyer
    Project Manager
    Form – Sample Development Contract

Chapter 15   Other Revenue / Support   159

   Introduction
   A Web Site
   Intranet
   E-Commerce
   External - Client Extras

Chapter 16   Purchases   161

   Introduction
   Desk and Chair
   Hardware and peripherals
   Software
   The Clients
   Library
   Old Hardware
   Old Software

Chapter 17   Building a History   165

   Introduction
   Design Specifications
   Design Specification Contracts
   Project Estimations – Before and After
   Design Specifications used by the developers
   Change Orders
   Issue Orders
   Employee Time Sheets
   Billing / Invoicing Information

Chapter 18   Plan – Business, Marketing and Sales 169

   Introduction
   Example Business Plan

Chapter 19   Customer Service   177

    Introduction
    Start at the beginning
    Sales Visits
    Meetings
    Design Specification
    Contracts
    Developing the Application
    Product Delivery
    Follow Up
    More

Chapter 20   Marketing and Sales   183

    Introduction
    Marketing
    Presenting Products and Services
    Here's what I would suggest
    Presenting Your Product as a Service
    News Releases
    Advertising, Marketing, and Communication
        Agencies
    Print Advertising
    Marketing Campaigns
    Mailing Lists
    Tailoring the message
    What lessons were learned?
    You're in the Door
    Explaining the Steps
    The First Contract

    The Second Contract
    Getting the Work Started

Chapter 21   Sales vs. Development   197

    Finding a Balance
    Prevention
    A Resolution
    Back to Work
    Divide and Conquer
    Visit
    The Final Decision
    Drop your Margin
    Fight
    Give It Up

Chapter 22   Document Responsibility   201

    The Project Book
    First Meeting Notes
    Continuing Meeting Notes
    Specification Writing Contract
    Specification Writing Notes
    Specification
    Estimate
    Application Development Contract
    Change Order
    Issue Order
    Developers Notes
    Developer's Specification
    Form – Chart of Responsibility

Chapter 23   Optimizing Jobs for Efficiency   207

    Introduction
    A Challenge
    The number of Jobs
    The length of Each Job
    Optimizing for Efficiency
    The Bottom line

Chapter 24	**Earning a Living Wage**	**211**
Chapter 25	**Managing Stress**	**213**
	Stress on the Developers	
	Stress on the Owner	
Chapter 26	**Risk**	**215**
Chapter 27	**Partners**	**217**
Chapter 28	**About the Author**	**219**

Chapter 1   Introduction

What Is This Book About?

The purpose of this book is to give your software development firm a leg up, not only on the competition, but also on the business practices necessary to make it more productive and more successful.

This is an advantage I wish we had when growing our firm. Everyday, for 15 years, I looked for something or someone that could provide me with a little bit of advice, answers a simple question, or point me in the right direction. I told myself that when I finally had the opportunity I would put it all down on paper. This book is the result.

To Whom Does This Book Speak?

I'm speaking to the software developer who wants to leave his current position and start his own firm. I'm speaking to the entrepreneur who has already started the business but wants to know what's ahead. I'm speaking to an owner and staff of a growing development firm who want to know how to handle more business.

A software development firm is a delicate balance between the art of design, the skill of development and the business world.

Delivering a piece of software on time and on budget and making a profit is not an accident. It is the product of finely tuned steps in the process.

What This Book Is Not

This book is not a technical manual. I am not recommending operating systems, development languages, or platforms. You know your technology better than anyone.

A Workbook

While writing, I realized that a manual like this can be a constant reference. Use it this way. Carry it with you, write notes, and make calculations on the pages. I have allowed room for your notes, thoughts, and comments throughout.

My Perspective

With all due respect to developers, technical writers, project managers, and administrative staff, I am writing this book from specific perspective. It is for the person or persons who are ultimately responsible for the success of the business.

A Final Note

I have been in this business for more than thirty years. It is important to remind owners and mangers of development firms that software developers are the heart of their business. If it were not for their long hours, their understanding of new technologies, and their continuing patience and dedication, there would be no software development firms to start, let alone grow.

• • •

Chapter 2   How to use this Book

Where to start reading!

The purpose of this book is to help you resolve everyday issues. Let me explain how I've broken the chapters down.

Chapters 3 & 4 are about your staff, hiring, and a discussion of how to structure your organization to get the most out of it.

Chapter 5 is a discussion of the cost of operating the business.

Chapter 6 is a discussion of the cost of administering the business.

Chapters 7 through 9 are a discussion of how to get the work done, from the design specification to developing the software.

Chapters 10 through 12 present tools that should be used while undertaking the work described in Chapters 5 through 7.

Chapters 13 through 15 address invoicing the customer. Your services are completed and you have earned payment...time to collect.

Chapter 16 is a brief discussion of office purchases. The business of software development can be an expensive proposition.

Chapter 17 discusses the considerations that you must make as a business owner once a project is complete and all the numbers are in.

Chapter 18 discusses writing a business plan and why it is so important.

Chapter 19 provides the reader with insight on customer service.

Chapter 20 considers the workings of your business, and includes a discussion on the external processes of sales and marketing.

Chapter 21 discusses the battles between the sales department and the developers.

Chapter 22 discusses who is responsible for each document.

Chapter 23 Optimizing jobs for efficiency.

Chapter 24 Earning a Living

Chapter 25 Managing Stress

Chapter 26 Risk

Chapter 27 Partners

Use this book however you see fit, starting where it might help the most and then move into the other chapters as you need them.

My suggestions are:

1. If you have not started your business yet then begin reading chapters 24 & 25. Next, move to chapters 2, 3, followed by chapters 4 through 16.

2. If your sales department is doing well already, but you are not making the margins you want, start with chapter 5 and read through to chapter 16.

3. If your business established and growth is something your next step, read chapter 18 on business plans.

4. If you are interested in documentation, its flow and who is responsible, focus on chapters 17 and 22.

5. Chapter 23 is about getting the most out of your workforce.

6. Chapters 24 – 27 are for you and your well being.

Project Flowchart

The chart that follows is the building block of this book. It is your visual roadmap of the entire project process, from very beginning to absolute end.

Chapter 2: How to use this Book

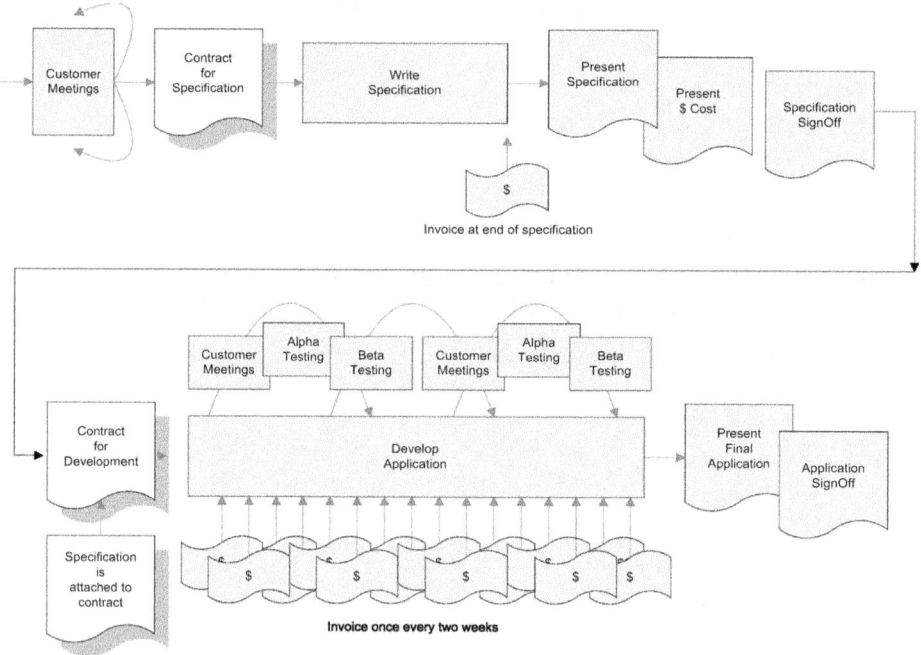

Chapter 3   The Staff

Introduction

Building a staff of developers, project managers and technical writers will be the most difficult part of your day-to-day operation. As much as you think you know, hiring an employee is always a gamble. Consider these things before you hire.

Personality of the Owner

Every boss, business owner, and entrepreneur has a unique personality. They are usually responsible for hiring developers themselves, and have a pre-conceived idea of what type of person they want. Always looking for the greatest employee will do you no good... they don't exist.

Business owners of software development firms make two mistakes the minute they open the doors. The first is they do the hiring with no help and the second is they hire people they're comfortable with. They both sound right and they're both wrong.

Think about it.

Human resource people don't start software development firms; technical people do. So how, all of a sudden, does a very technical business owner become an expert in human resources?

I know it is exciting to hire that first person, but consider the ramifications of making a mistake so early in the life of your organization. The earlier you hire the wrong person, the harder it will be to recover. Slow down.

If you are in the early stages of growth and do not have anyone to turn to on the inside, find someone on the outside. Ask for their help in the interviewing process. They may not understand technical issues, but allow them to get a feel for the other important factors such as communication skills, maturity, and personality. Then consider the whole picture, and make a decision based on both.

A common mistake

Look in the mirror some early morning and consider the fact that you may be trying to hire the person looking back at you. It is a scary thought isn't it?

Everyone tends to hire people they are comfortable with. That means they hire people with similar skills, speech patterns, or interests. Keep in mind that you are hiring a person that will help you develop your business. The ability to take direction, go the extra mile, perform in front of customers, and communicate is invaluable. Don't clone yourself; compliment yourself by adding skills for both your business and your technology.

[A Comment: I've always let more senior developers interview a prospective employee. Because I could not always have to keep up on the new technologies, it paid off from both a skills and morale perspective to have other employed do the interviewing.]

Personality of the team

The personality of the people you hire will directly effect whether or not you succeed. You will find over time that the dynamics within your organization will become strong and active. The sooner you understand, accept, and work with them, the more you will accomplish.

The Operation and Management of a Software Company

[A Story: The second office I moved into had a lot of nice small offices with doors that shut. Every staff member had plenty of space and cabinets to fill up and room to spread out. The office was glass, brass and doors shut. Work was getting done but there wasn't the energy I wanted.

When it was time to move into a larger office I realized I had made a lot of mistakes in the previous layout so I adjusted the new space. The new office was one big open area with large round desks. Each desk could accommodate three staff members. Each workspace, within each desk, had a nice leather chair, phone, room for books and a stereo (with headphones of course), but most importantly, with a view of each other. The energy instantly went up. At each desk we placed a new hire, a developer that had been with us awhile and a technical writer or project manager. Not only did mentoring start across the desk but from desk to desk. Our teams began working together more than ever before. The dynamics of support and cross training was not something I could have mandated.]

[A Comment: A couple interesting notes on the open layout. From a distance I could always tell who wasn't going to fit in. The open layout forced the staff to step up and communicate and some employees could not manage it. Another benefit was that everyone was aware of any issues or problems. Hidden agendas do not have a very long life span in an open office.]

How to locate, interview, hire and build a development staff

Locating personnel

As the economy changes so does supply of staff members. I have successfully found technical people by four different methods. They are:

Referrals: I suggest a policy of rewarding your staff for recommended new hires, once they pass the evaluation period.

Internet: The internet has always worked best. Reasonable costs and worldwide exposure can only help. Be selective in the employment sites you use. Ask, where do the type of developers I need, look for employment?

Newspaper: Newspapers are a lot less useful than they used to be. With access to the Internet, newspapers just aren't cost effective.

Headhunters: This method is the least productive and most expensive. With a little effort and use of your staff you can review the same résumé's, select the candidates and interview without having to pay the enormous finders fees.

[A Comment: A $60,000 developer can cost you upwards of $15,000 in fees. That's 150 hours at $100 an hour. It shouldn't cost that much.]

Interviewing personnel

Interviewing a prospective employee should be a team effort allowing for a well-rounded review of the candidate. Allow one or more in-house staff members, based on their skills, to do a portion of each interview.

In addition you may want to ask the candidate to take a one or more skill tests. There are wide varieties of tests available for purchase and use. One method that has been proven to work quite well is

The Operation and Management of a Software Company 11

to ask the candidate to take one of the standards test given by Microsoft or other software companies. The person can be directed to a local testing facility and asked to return the test score immediately after taking the test.

If you're interested in digging deeper into the person's abilities there are a wide range of personality tests that can help.

[A Story: One thing I did was to ask a local psychologist, which handles this type of work force analysis, to create a standardized test that would determine if the prospective employee's personality traits would match the overall personality of our current team of developers.

Once the test was created we had all the current developers take the test, creating a standard single profile. We then asked all prospective employees, which we believed were close to being hired, to take the test, voluntarily of course. We judged the results against the norm and made our determination.]

Once the interview is completed it's recommended that the interview team sit down and critique the candidate. Even with more candidates to interview, reviewing each individually, as soon as possible, will help you make a better decision.

Handbook

One important item that you should have is a handbook. It makes it a lot easier to deal with the day-to-day issues if you get it down once in document form.

I have attached an example at the end of this chapter.

Hiring Your Staff

There are several recommended steps in hiring the candidates you've selected. The steps are:

1. Provide them with a Letter of Intent disclosing all agreed upon parameters. Leave nothing out. If you leave something out now it will inevitably come back to haunt you.

2. Prior to the first day of work provide the candidate with company policies and employment agreements. Allow them to discuss any issues they may have. Address the concerns as quickly and as straightforwardly as possible.

[A Story: I know of one firm that actually forgot to tell a new employee that the first two weeks of their pay were held back and that in effect they weren't going to get paid until the first month of work was completed. Not a good way to start a relationship.]

3. Prior to the new employee's arrival determine where the person will sit, the correct hardware and software setup. Select a mentor, and pre-schedule several days, if not weeks, of introductions, training and work. Trying to schedule on the fly only detracts from everyone else's workload. Do it before the candidate arrives and efficiency won't be lost.

4. Upon arrival accomplish the final document signings, introductions, seating, etc. Too often developers are set down and left to their own

resources. It doesn't work, it's unproductive and it's the new employees chance to see how unorganized you are.

Building a Staff

Building a staff that works well together is a time consuming effort. Everything we've talked supports that effort but you must always keep in mind the bigger picture. Not only are you hiring a specific skill set but you are also hiring a person that fits into the larger scheme of things, a person that is, among other things, comfortable in front of customers, can write and speak in a professional manner and is willing to put in the effort that you're going to ask from them.

Also keep in mind that as you grow you're going to ask some of the people you've hired to move out of their skill set and into management roles. It's important that you always hire staff with the implied expectation that they are going to move up to positions with broader responsibilities.

[A Comment: Moving a person from a technical role into a management role doesn't always work. Too often I have seen absolutely great developers moved into management because they were doing a great job... at development. I've often had to be reminded that just because you can write code doesn't mean you can manage people. I would suggest letting the technical people tell you where they want to go and then support and train them for advancement as you would a developer on new skills.]

Additional Skills

As has been said the better rounded the individual employee, the greater your reach is going to be. What's meant by reach is that the more skills the individual employee brings with them or is trained for, the more you're going to be able to accomplish with the workforce. So, what are some of the other skill sets that you need to look for?

Communications

It sounds almost too simple. The person you hire must be able to communicate with those around them, on the phone, and with customers. If they can't do this right from the start you can't use them, no matter how good they may be at everything else.

[A Story: I hired a young man that was absolutely great technologically. He had written software for 5 years in a wide number of languages, had several degrees, and did well when interviewed by our senior developers. The problem was that when it came to speaking to anyone outside the technical community he just couldn't get across his ideas. Our customers didn't speak Visual Basic. He couldn't put a business sentence together to save this life. It was an expensive mistake on my part.]

Emotional Maturity

This may seem an odd skill to be concerned about but it's an important part of a complete employee. When working in a stressful environment such as software development, if you can't handle pressure this is the last business you want be in.

[A Story: In the mid 1990's I had an employee actually sit down in the open hall of a Big Six's corporate headquarters and cried. I understood the pressure they were under to deliver the product but the client didn't.]

Reading and Writing

All too often I've found the critical reading and writing skills needed to blend a technical discipline into a business environment have been lacking. This is not to say that our staff lacked the standard capacities to read and write but often lacked the ability to translate what they knew into a form that our customers could use and understand.

To remedy this situation we moved this process into the mentoring program. Every time something had to be written or presented we worked with the newer employees to help develop them.
The practice worked well.

Dressing the Part

Technical people, whether they believe it or not, must be presentable in front of customers. The rule of thumb that I've always used is that our people must dress at least to the level of the customer they're dealing with. In the office they were allowed to dress causally but were asked to have a change of clothes in the closet.

It also became apparent early on that many of our young staff members didn't know how to dress once asked. To remedy this I went out and purchased two wonderful books, one for men and women on how to dress and put a wardrobe together. As much as no one wanted to admit it, it seemed to help. It is titled "Men's Wardrobe". Kim Johnson Gross and Jeff Stone wrote it. Alfred A. Knopf Publisher, New York, published it.

[A Story: On the exact same day I had an employee drop to the floor and start crying I had another who, when asked for the first time to visit the same client site, wore what could only be described as a 20 year old prom dress. Some days you're just going to need a sense of humor!]

The ability to understand business

If you can get your staff to understand the makeup of your business and how it truly works you're going to be much better off. Most developers do not come with a sense of how business operates, as a whole, let alone a unique business like development. I might suggest that once you finish this book you pass it to your staff.

[A Story: In mid 1997 our business was really on an upturn and I needed more developers. I decided to interview students from surrounding colleges hoping to win them over before they graduated. In walked this kid. We went through the regular interview but I noticed that he was asking more and more questions. As I finished he took over. He explained he had done his homework and that in his college town he was worth $ 38,000 a year. In another city nearby he was worth $35,000. He then explained that he was willing to take $36,000 to work for us because his family was near. Talk about understanding how things work. I hired him before he left the building.]

Selecting Software Developers

As a development shop owner you know the technical aspects for determining the skills of a developer. We've talked about the other skills they should have, but most importantly make sure that he or she is more than just a development language. I can't say this enough; the more well rounded the person is, the more you're going to be able to do with that person and the further they're going to go. Make sure he brings assets that you don't have and that will help grow the business over the next several years.

Selecting Technical Writers

Beyond the standard skills of a technical writer, this staff member needs to be a real communicator. Often they're the first one into a customer's site after the sales person. They'll be the one that begins building the relationship and quite often will continue that relationship for years to come. The customer will identify them as the one that really understands their business. Your technical writer will often be the one called upon when there's more work, which makes them a sales person, on occasion.

Selecting Project Managers

Aside from all the professional skills a project manager comes with he also needs to be a negotiator and leader. This staff member is, in the end, the one that not only makes a successful project but the one that motivates and retains the developers you've worked so hard to hire.

How the three skill sets work together

The Project Manager – PM: This person is brought in immediately upon the signing of the development contract with the client. The PM is introduced to the client. It's explained that he's the focal point for all communications and questions as the project moves forward.

The Technical Writer – TW: If a project needs technical documentation such as a design specification or users manual, the technical writer is brought in to work directly with the customer to create the documentation necessary.

The Software Developer: One or more software developers are assigned to a project based on the size and scope of the project.

To understand how to hire any one of these three skill sets outside of their technical qualifications, you need to understand that these people work together every day and to do so they need the ability to work as a team.

1. The PM must be very organized and have the ability to understand and work with the client, the technical writer and the developer while at the same time leading them all in the same direction. The PM must be able to do this and at the same time make sure that the business side of the equation is satisfied. The PM is like a general contractor, all knowing and ultimately responsible. The PM needs the complete cooperation of the management staff, the customer, the technical writer, and the developers.

2. The Technical Writer must be able to communicate in one direction and write a document in the other. It isn't an easy thing to do. They need to get the client to express their needs in such a way that he can take those needs and write them down in a useable form, for both the client and the developer.

I've always explained the specification document to our clients by saying that they could read it and know exactly what we're going to build for them and the developer can read the same document and not have to ask the client or the technical writer what was meant to be built. Quite often it's a difficult task to accomplish but a good technical writer can get it done. The technical writer is the architect, responsible for design and blueprints but gets little of the final credit. The TW needs the cooperation of the customer, and the developers.

3. The developer is the builder. He's handed a specification, a set of blueprints if you will, and is told to go off and make everyone else look good. His position is to take the ideas expressed on paper, filtered through the technical writer, and make them functional.

In the best of all worlds the developer now has everything necessary to do his job and needs little cooperation from the others. In the real world the developer will ask questions everyday, which if the TW can't answer, the PM must.

The structure of a development environment

From practical experience I believe the development environment needs to be an open, supportive, and academic. What I mean by academic is an office that believes in computer science, software development, and the learning and professional growth of the staff. It should be a place that fosters growth and opportunity, with ability to learn more than imagined. Ultimately they need to know that the time spent with your company is well spent.

[A Story: Sometimes you can't win for losing. I had an employee that walked in one morning and explained that he was quitting. No notice at all. When I asked where he was going he explained that he had promised the customer, my customer that he would start working for them, as an employee, the very next morning.]

I'll explain it another way just in case this seems too weird. A customer of mine hired away one of our employees while that employee was working on a job for them and the customer expected the employee to quit that Tuesday evening and start with them on a Wednesday morning AND both the employee and the customer had signed more than one agreement that they could not do what they had just done!

I'll add to the story. When I told the employee that he could quit any time though he had agreed to a two weeks notice he could not go to the customer as an employee because he had contracted not to, as did the customer. You know what my ex-employee did? He got mad at me! He said I had earned enough money off of him. That it was his decision. That my asking him to adhere to the contracts he had signed and earned a good living off of just wasn't fair!

All I can say is, no matter how hard you try and how many flags you send up, it not always going to work out.]

How to get the most from your staff

I am a big proponent of the open office layout. Not because it was a fad but because I've seen how it works to everyone's advantage. Let me explain the advantages;

1. The most obvious, from a management point of view, is that you can see everything that's happening in the office. Who's late, who working, and who needs help. More importantly your team can see you. They need to know you're there and interested.

[A Comment: I manage by walking around so this layout allowed me to practice the style of management I enjoyed.]

2. It builds a team approach. As much as technical people are very individualistic, it is important that this layout be used as a mechanism to create a single coherent team.

3. Without individual offices mentoring is possible. You can place the rookies with more seasoned personnel. Whether you use flat square tables or large round ones you'll have the ability to place a person where it'll do you and them the most good.

   [A Comment: The open space layout worked better than even imagined. We were bringing in new developers that within a few months were mentoring others. Consider this when hiring. Can this person move fast enough to mentor others?]

4. The open space layout allows you the ability to create teams that can physically sit together. If a project calls for three programmers, a technical writer, and a project manager you can pull them all together into one team, into one space. This increases the level of responsibility the team members have to each other and doesn't allow anyone to back off.

5. Communications will go up. I don't mean the kind that distracts, but the kind that enlighten and support the progress of the personnel and the projects they work on.

   [A Story: When I first started out I had the developers build libraries to store code snippets, as they found new ways of doing things. In our closed-door offices the library never got used. The closed doors just weren't conducive to sharing immediate information. In the open layout the developer continued to store code in the library but they would also look across the table and tell their team members what they had just done. We decreased our development time.]

Managing a development workforce

There is an absolute mountain of books on management styles. You may want to consult a few or maybe you've already developed your own, but no matter how you work with your staff there are some things that you need to understand and appreciate.

1. Your staff is very proud of their work. Much like the builder of a home, when the keys are passed to the new owner the builder is still very proud of that house.

2. Because of this pride the staff will be very defensive about their work. Respect their position. Understand that developers are very close in sentiment to artists. This thing they're building, no matter who is paying for it, is their baby.

3. Your staff will work long hours to complete a task. Make sure that if they're taking care of you, you take care of them. See Below.

4. Your staff wants to learn as much as they can and quite often as fast as they can. Make sure that you give them an environment that addresses this issue.

Don't forget that your employees have needs above and beyond your business and if you can help them satisfy those needs you're going to have a workforce that stands behind you.

Let me list some of the things we did that I believe made a difference.

1. Our office was in a highly congested office complex and mall. During December each year we allowed the staff to leave in the middle of the day to shop for Christmas. The stipulation was that they had to work the lost hours on the same day.

2. We located consigners services that picked up their laundry.

3. Every Friday we had lunch together to discuss any and all questions.

4. Flex hours if you can make them work.

5. A developer's forum was created to discuss software development issues, both personal and professional.

6. A kitchen was put in so that the staff didn't always have to run out for lunch in colder weather.]

[A Story; after I sold my business in late 2000 I got an email invitation. It was to be Friday evening at one of the local restaurants. It was a gathering of all my old employees, as far back as the days when I started the business in the basement. Apparently my employees had been holding a sort of an alumni party once a year, and I had never known it.

I think it says a lot about the people, the relationship to each other, and the environment they created for themselves in the work place.

I hope they enjoyed working for the firm as much as I enjoyed having them as friends.]

Reporting Structure

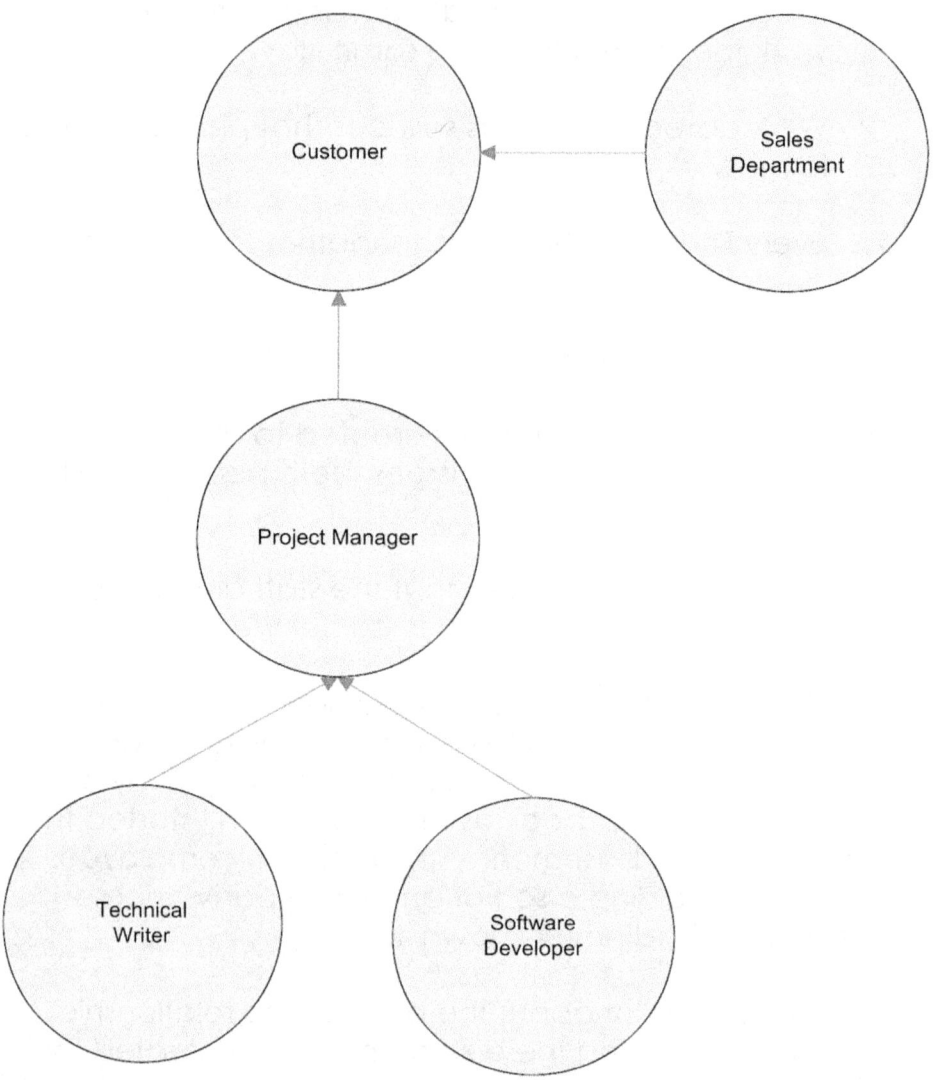

Your Company's Employee Handbook

WELCOME to ………….., Inc.

I am pleased to have you join us and hope that you will enjoy working with us. This Employee handbook outlines some of the privileges and benefits which the company currently offers and explains some of your responsibilities as an employee. You are required to read this Handbook carefully so that you will be aware of the Company's current policies, benefits, and procedures. This Handbook is only a general guide to the Company's current employment policies and to some of your benefits and responsibilities as an employee. It is informational only and is not intended to be nor should it be construed as a contract. The Company from time to time reviews its policies, procedures, and benefits and makes revisions based upon the need for and desirability of changes. Thus, any policy, procedure, or benefit outlined in this Manual may be modified, increased, or decreased at any time, with or without advance notice, and you may not rely on any policies that have been superseded.

If you have any questions, The Human Resources Department will be glad to answer them.

Your employment relationship with the Company is entered into voluntarily and you are free to resign at any time. Similarly, the Company is free to conclude the employment relationship at any time for any reason, subject to the terms and conditions of the Employment Agreement.

This Employee Handbook supersedes all previous Employee Handbooks and any memos, which may have been issued or posted on subjects covered in this handbook.

Good Luck and best wishes to you.

……………….., President

Your Company, Inc. Mission Statement

To provide the highest quality software solutions in the industry.

Business Attitude

Customer Service

Nothing comes before customer service. We will give the customer not only the service they expect but even more than expected. I want the customer surprised and please with everything we do for them, no less. The bottom line is to treat the customer, as we want to be treated, if we were in their place.

Accountability

If service is first, accountability is second. When it comes to our customers and the cost of quality software we are 100% accountable. To our customers there are no excuses and we will make none. Every employee of ....is a professional and professionals are responsible for "all" of their work.

Quality

Quality means delivering the software product ordered, on time, within budget, to the customer's satisfaction.

Speed

Speed means getting things done at worst case on time. Speed means calling the customer sooner. Speed means delivering cleaner code earlier. Haste wins customers.

Action

Action means being proactive. Our customer service, our quality, our speed and accountability must be proactive. We do not wait for an answer we go find it. We do not merely satisfy the customer but please them. We do not move at the speed of our competitors but faster.

The more proactive we are the more customers we'll satisfy and retain over the long term.

Employee Status

Regular Employees

Regular Status: An employee that is expected to work a minimum of 40 hours per week.

Intern Status: An employee that is hired and works a varied number of hours per week, with no guarantee of obtaining 'Regular' employee status.

Non-Regular Part Time Employees: An employee that works a non-regular schedule at less than 40 hours per week.

Temporary Employees: An employee that works for a stated amount of time with ...., Inc. Hours can range from 1 to 40 hours.

Salary and Hourly

There are two types of employee payment types at ...., Inc., salary and hourly. All professional developers and networking personnel are salaried and shall work no less than 40 hours per week, but shall not have a limit above 40 hours per week, as the job requires. All other personnel, at management's discretion, are hourly employees.

Hourly Employee Time Sheets

Hourly Employee Time sheets are to be delivered to their supervisor by 12 noon on every Thursday prior to payday.

Salary Time Sheets

>Time Sheets are to be entered on the ....
>Intranet timesheet program on a daily basis.

Education

>Outside education is encouraged and allowed. It is the employee's responsibility to inform his/her supervisor prior to making firm arrangements and it is the supervisor's responsibility to make every effort to allow the employee to continue their education.

Keeping Current

>All employees are expected to keep current in their line of expertise. This is to be accomplished by reading and/or reviewing the technical journals provided by the company. It is also accomplished by attending required classes, which the Management expects you to go to.

Work Schedule - Hours of Work

>All employees work a standard 40-hour week from 8am - 5pm, Monday through Friday. However, to continue to provide quality support to our customers, it will be necessary for professional personnel to work evenings, nights, and weekends, as a project requires.

Meal Periods

>Lunches are to be taken from 12 noon until 1pm. It is understood that exceptions are necessary. If the lunch period is moved from the required, please notify your supervisor.

Breaks

If workload allows and working conditions warrant, employees are granted one 10-minute paid break during any work period of four consecutive hours. Breaks are a privilege and may not be added to meal periods, used to shorten the workday, or take in conjunction with any type of leave.

Reporting Absences from Work

You must promptly report all absences from work to your supervisor directly. Do not leave voice or email mail unless you can't get a hold of anyone on the phone. If you are going to be late or unable to attend due to illness, notify your supervisor before the start of the workday or as soon as possible. If you are going to be absent more than one day, you must talk to your supervisor. Employees failing to report absences for three consecutive days may be separated from employment as a voluntary resignation.

Attendance and Punctuality:

Policy: It is the policy of ...., Inc. to require good attendance and punctuality on the part of its employees. Unauthorized or excessive absences or tardiness will not be tolerated and may result in disciplinary action, and/or termination.

Employees should notify their supervisor, as far in advance as possible whenever they are unable to report for work or know they will be late. Such notification should include a reason for the absence or lateness and an indication of when the employee can be expected to report for work. Failure to notify the ...., Inc. of any absence or delay may be grounds for disciplinary action.

Non-exempt employees: Failure to notify the ...., Inc. of any absence or delay will normally result in loss of compensation during the absence or delay and may be grounds for disciplinary action.

Storm Days: Employees are expected to report for work during inclement weather conditions if ...., Inc. does not declare an emergency closing.

Non-exempt employees: Those employees who are unable to report because of weather conditions will be granted an authorized unpaid absence, or at the employee's request, one vacation day. Employees who are late because of weather conditions will be given a chance to make up their missed time if work schedules and conditions permit.

Adverse Weather

Employees must account for any work time lost by adverse weather. This is true whether the company closes, individual departments close, an employee leaves work early, an employee does not report to work due to transportation difficulties, etc.

Non-exempt employees: To account for lost time, either vacation leave must be charged, or subject to supervisory approval, the time may be made up. If lost time is not made up with a 6-month period, it must be charged as leave.

If it becomes necessary for an employee to remain away from work because of illness, accident, or other reason, the supervisor must be notified promptly. Absences without notification to the supervisor are grounds for dismissal.

Other Employment

Positions with ...., Inc., if you are a regular employee, are considered primary employment. The outside job must not conflict with the satisfactory performance of your regular duties or be in a field, which is considered in competition with ...., Inc. No employee may engage, directly or indirectly in any form, as an employee, contractor, independent contractor, agent, or otherwise for any person, firm, corporation or any business which directly or indirectly competes with ...., Inc. or for any past or present account of ...., Inc. or to engage in providing service for compensation or otherwise in the field of employment at ...., Inc.

Dress Code

Since we are a consulting company, there are times that employees must work at a client's site. Therefore, the dress code should be appropriate to the dress of the clients.

Everyone should also have the appropriate dress on site at all times in case you are called out to a clients site without prior notice. This includes a shirt, tie, slacks, etc.

Ask your supervisor for specific situations.

First and foremost company policy is to always be prepared for the customer. If you are not dressed for a particular situation, the appropriate clothing must be at hand to do so. Storage will be provided on-site.

..............., Inc. Office Attire:

Monday through Thursday, each employee' dress code is "Business Casual".

Business Casual is:

Men; Dress pants / Dockers or Chinos. Dress or polo shirts (such as a .... shirt). Shirts must have a collar. Tie is optional but must be readily available for dress shirts. Appropriate shoes, soft shoes or tennis shoes are not appropriate

<u>Ladies</u>; Dress pants / skirt or dress. Blouse or polo shirts (such as a .... shirt). Appropriate shoes, soft shoes or tennis shoes are not appropriate.

Client Site:

It is important to dress at the level of our client or one notch up, but absolutely never less than our clients are.

Friday will be a casual day. Casual Fridays are to relax from the formal dress of the week but to still set the correct presentation for the office. Dress will include jeans, collared shirts, sneakers, etc. However cutoffs are not appropriate. Use good judgement so that it is business appropriate. Abuse of casual day my lead to the removal of casual day.

The bottom line is that everyone at .... is a professional software developer and a consultant. Our clients must receive the level of professionalism they expect for the price they pay and our presentation is very much a part of that professionalism.

Smoking

Smoking will only be allowed in outside, designated smoking areas.

Confidentiality

See the Employment Agreement

Use of Company Property, Equipment, Resources

............, Inc. employees may not use ...., Inc. property or funds for personal gain or personal purposes. This includes, but is not limited to, telephones, equipment, or mail services. Misuse of company property or funds may result in dismissal.

Solicitation

Employees may not sell or promote the sale of any goods or services for personal gain on company property. Also groups or individuals that are not affiliated with the company are prohibited from selling or promoting the sale of goods or services on company property without written permission.

Use of Mail and Telephones

The company mail system is for handling official company mail. Employees should not use it for personal correspondence. Personal phone calls are occasionally necessary. However, at no time may long distance phone calls or toll calls of a personal nature be made at the company's expense.

Use of Email

> The company email system is for handling official company email. Employees should not use it for personal correspondence. Personal email is occasionally necessary. However, at no time may email charges of a personal nature be created at the company's expense.

Use of Internet

> The company Internet system is for handling official company business. It is not for personal use, except for allowable 'browsing' on the employees lunch period. However, at no time may Internet charges of a personal nature be created at the company's expense.

Computer Security

> Computer security is of the utmost importance to ...., Inc. and it's clients, and at not time is any information, passwords, phone numbers, etc. to be given to any party, inside or outside ...., Inc. Each individual employee is responsible for their phone numbers and passwords and the security that those pieces of information provide. The inability to maintain personal and corporate security will be grounds for immediate dismissal.

Building Security

> Employees are supplied with keys and passwords, allowing them to enter the premises in off-hours. This is to be considered a very important responsibility and is to be treated as such.

Upon arriving on off-hours, said employee(s) is responsible for the .... facility while present. As well once inside the building all external doors are to be kept locked.

Upon leaving on off-hours, said employee(s) is responsible to check all doors, lights - off air conditioners - appropriate, and any other internal building function that would cause discomfort or harm to .... and or its employee(s). Employee is responsible for setting the alarm.

Failure to follow appropriate procedure will be considered grounds for disciplinary action.

Nondiscrimination Policy

.... is dedicated to equality of opportunity within its community and supports the protection available to its employees and applicants under federal law. Accordingly the company does not practice or condone discrimination in any form and is committed to positive action to secure equal opportunity regardless of race, color, national origin, religion, sex, age, or disability.

Maintaining a Drug-Free Workplace

An employee who reports to work under the influence of illegal drugs or who uses drugs on the job may be dismissed without prior warning. Drug abuse by employees may subject them to criminal prosecution by government agencies, in addition to disciplinary action by the company.

Employees who suspect that they may have a drug problem are encouraged to seek help.

Alcohol Policy

The consumption or possession of alcoholic beverages on …… Property or while on ………… business, except for officially sanctioned functions or storage locations, is prohibited. Supervisory personnel must approve any exception to this policy for special occasions.

Off the job use of alcohol, which adversely affects an employees job performance, which has an effect on …………, Inc. or which jeopardizes the safety or property of other employees, customers, or the public is discouraged. Employees are prohibited from reporting to work under the influence.

In addition, persons whose positions with ………… require driving as part of their work may be removed or terminated from such position if found to have been driving under the influence of alcohol while on duty.

Employees who suspect that they may have an alcohol problem are encouraged to seek help.

Sexual harassment

All employees are guaranteed the right to work in an environment free from sexual harassment. Sexual harassment is defined as deliberate, unsolicited, and unwelcome verbal or physical conduct of a sexual nature or with sexual implications which, when accepted or rejected, may have direct employment consequences. Such conduct has the intention or effect of unreasonable interfering with an individual's work performance or of creating an intimidating, hostile, or offensive working environment. Personal compliments welcomed by the recipient and social interaction freely entered into are not considered sexual harassment.

The management of ...., Inc. strictly forbids any form of sexual harassment, directly or indirectly, and any incident of sexual harassment is to be reported to management immediately.

Employee Purchasing Procedure

All and any purchases made for, or by ...., Inc. must be authorized by a company officer(s). Failure to do so will place burden of product(s) cost on purchaser.

Travel

Meals - Meals are not afforded to the employee by the company. The employee must pick up cost of own meal unless otherwise stated by the .... – Client contract.

Mileage - .... will cover standard 0.325 cents per mile to the client site and back based on Federal regulation for allowable charges.

Parking - .... will cover reasonable parking charges.

Over Night - Meals - Over nights are not afforded to the employee by the company. The employee must pick up cost of own stay unless otherwise stated by the .... -- Client contract. This depends on the situation.

Employee Relations

Discipline

> We intend to take a constructive approach to disciplinary matters to insure that actions, which would interfere with operations or an employee's job, are not continued.
>
> Commission of any of the following acts will subject an employee to disciplinary action, up to and including discharge:

1. Failure to perform job assignments satisfactorily and efficiently.

2. Supplying false or misleading information or withholding requested information when applying for employment.

3. Unauthorized publication of confidential information.

4. Engaging in such other practices as may be inconsistent with the ordinary and reasonable rules of conduct necessary to the welfare of the company and its employees.

5. Smoking, eating, or drinking in unauthorized areas.

6. Malingering, loitering, or sleeping on the job.

7. Interfering with, defacing, changing, or altering any posted work schedule, employee notice, directive, or order. Posting notices contrary to company policy.

The Operation and Management of a Software Company

8. Failure to keep your work area neat and clean at all times.

9. Entering or using company property without permission.

10. Roughhousing

11. Failure to report unsafe actions or conditions.

12. Theft or misappropriation of customer, employee, or company property. Unauthorized removal of any of the above including items found on the premises. Lost items that are found by employees must be turned into their supervisor immediately.

13. Unauthorized possession of firearms, explosives, or any other dangerous weapons on company premises while performing company duties.

14. Reporting to work under the influence of intoxicants or illegal drugs.

15. Drinking alcoholic beverages, using illegal drugs, or possessing either on company time or premises.

16. Refusing to allow examination of the contents of locker or incoming or outgoing boxes, parcels, lunch pails, pockets, etc.

17. Provoking or instigating a fight with another employee or any other person during working hours on company property.

18. Malicious misuse, destruction, or damage of any company or the property of any employee or customer.

19. Failure to report any personal injury, no matter how small, immediately to your supervisor.

20. Unexcused tardiness.

21. Solicitations of other employees or customers for any reason or distribution of literature of any kind during work hours or in work areas.

22. Failure to comply with the company's rules of safety and work dress.

23. Mishandling of company funds or intentional misdirection of company business.

24. Use of company material, time or equipment, for an unauthorized purpose or personal use.

25. Insubordination or refusal to comply with instructions or failure to perform assigned.

26. Performance which, in the company's opinion, does not meet the requirements or standards of the position.

27. Other circumstance in which the company feels that discipline is warranted.

This list is intended to be representative of the types of activities which may result in disciplinary action. It is not intended to be comprehensive and does not alter the employment-at-will relationship between the employee and the company.

Resolving Employee Concerns

Employee Concerns can be taken to the employee's supervisor and/or the Human Resources Manager.

Disruptive Conduct

Disruptive behavior, defined as behavior not standard for a professional office demeanor, will not be tolerated and the employee will be considered for disciplinary action, including dismissal.

Employee Paycheck

Pay Practices

Paychecks are presented to employees the Friday after the completed pay period. Non-Exempt employees must have their hours into the accounting office by the preceding Thursday by 12 noon, prior to the payday.

Direct Deposit

Direct deposit is available. A form must be filled out and it will take 10 days to be effective.

Paycheck Deductions

See accounting office for any deductions.

Lost/Stolen Checks

Please notify ...., Inc. accounting as quickly as possible. ....is not accountable for lost or stolen checks.

Overtime

> Salaried employees are not paid overtime. Hourly employees are paid overtime.

Jury Duty

> Employees will be granted jury duty leave with no loss in regular wages.

Bereavement Leave

> ...., Inc. recognizes the need for absence because of a death in the family. In the event the death is of a member of the immediate family, a three-day absence shall be automatically granted without loss of pay. If the deceased is a relative outside of the immediate family, the employee shall be excused, with pay, on the day of the funeral. It is further recognized that in some cases this is not sufficient time to handle necessary details and in such cases additional unpaid days may be authorized with the approval of the Supervisor.

Leave of Absence

> An unpaid leave of absence may be requested for medical leave, or military leave, and, if approved by the Supervisor, will be granted for a period of not more than 6 months, except as required by law. During this period no vacation or sick time will be accrued and arrangements must be made with the Human Resources Office for payment of medical, dental, life insurance and long term disability insurance premiums to ensure continued coverage of these benefits.

Employee Time Off

Paid Holidays

For full-time employees:

1. New Years Day
2. Memorial Day
3. 4th of July
4. Labor Day
5. Thanksgiving
6. Christmas or Hanukkah

Vacation Leave

..............., Inc. policy is:

1-week paid vacation <u>after</u> 1 year has been completed.

2-weeks paid vacation <u>after</u> 2 years have been completed.

3-weeks paid vacation <u>after</u> 5 years have been completed.

Sick Leave

Regular Full-time Employees:

All full-time year round employees are eligible to be compensated for sick leave depending on when the employee starts.

January 1st – March 31st 3 sick days

April 1st – July 31st 2 sick days

August 1st – December 31st

    1 sick day

Any leave not used during the year will be lost. Payment will not be made for any unused sick time.

Sick leave may be used for the following reasons **only**:

    a. Illness of employee
    b. Illness of family member
    c. Medical and Dental appointments

It is Management's discretion to ask for a doctor's excuse. Abuse of this policy may result in disciplinary action.

If all sick leave is exhausted, vacation leave will be charged for any additional time taken.

If all leave (both sick and vacation leave) has been exhausted, consideration will be given for the advancement of up to 40 hours of additional unpaid time under the following conditions:

    Compelling circumstances (i.e., catastrophic illness or circumstances)

        The approval of the department supervisor (and department Manager, if applicable)

        The time advanced will be deducted from future accruals of sick and vacation leave.

If sick and vacation leave are both exhausted, then an unpaid leave of absence may be requested for a period up to 6 months.

The Operation and Management of a Software Company

Personal Days

Regular Full-time Employees:

All full-time year round employees are eligible to be compensated for personal leave depending on when the employee starts.

January 1st – March 31st
3 personal days

April 1st – July 31st
2 personal days

August 1st – December 31st
1 personal day

Any leave not used during the year will be lost. Payment will not be made for any unused personal time.

Retirement Plan 401K

Medical Insurance Plan

The Company has available Group Medical Insurance, which includes a $10,000 Life Insurance policy. The cost of insurance is split; the Company pays 50% and the employee 50%.

For more details please see the accounting department.

Dental Insurance Plan

The Company has available Group Dental Insurance. The cost of insurance is split; the Company pays 50% and the employee 50%.

For more details please see the accounting department.

Disability Insurance Plan L/T and S/T

The Company has available long-term and short-term disability. The cost of insurance is split; the Company pays 50% and the employee 50%.

For more details please see the accounting department.

Office Rules

The new office is designed significantly different than the Canton office with space being presented quite differently. Therefore we are going to need to adjust how we operate.

1. With the open office, we will all need to show a lot of respect for the other person's privacy, work space and work focus. Any discussions must be moved to one of the several conference rooms.

2. All personal phone calls are to be made from a conference room, for your privacy as well as for those around you.

3. All coats and such will be hung in front lobby closet.

4. Lunches are to be stored in lunchroom.

5. If you eat lunch in, lunches are to be eaten in the lunchroom, not at your desk.

The Operation and Management of a Software Company

6. Desks will need to be kept neat and organized. Please do it before you leave each day.

7. Stereos and radios are allowed but please use headphones.

8. At the end of the day all dishes are to be returned to the kitchen and dishwasher if necessary.

9. Last person out of the office sets alarm, as in Canton.

10. Last person out starts up the dishwasher.

11. We have a stove in the kitchen. If you use it, please clean it and put dishes in dishwasher immediately.

12. Please use appropriate caution when in the office by yourself. Please keep the front door locked after hours.

13. Please use appropriate caution when leaving the office after hours. An alarm is available to carry with you. Office complex police are also available to escort you. Please use these services.

Customer Management – in the ....office

The proper management of customers, while in our offices, is very important to .... Our offices are not only a place for us to do our work but also as a marketing tool, an image, presented to our customers and / or potential customers.

With this in mind, this document will provide the standards by which customers must be handled. It is the responsibility of the most senior person, supporting the customer, to see that the following items are taken are of.

1. Schedule the meeting room with Kim
2. Advise Kim as to the refreshments that are to be provided.
3. See that the location for the meeting is clean and stocked with all supplies necessary for the meeting. Advise Kim as to what is not available
4. Advise / Email "All" as to the meeting allowing all staff to maintain proper decorum while the customer is on-site. Location of meeting can be anywhere that you believe the customer is comfortable and the surrounding add to the meeting, whether that is the server room, the conference rooms or the couches.
5. An agenda must be provided, no matter how brief, to the customer and attending .... employees.
6. If collateral material is to be presented to the customer, it must be presented in document form and not just verbally.
7. Notes of the meeting must be kept and attached to agenda once completed.
8. No meeting should be completed without a final discussion of the "Next Steps". These next steps must be attached to the agenda along with the meeting notes.

These steps are really quite simple but allow a structure to the visits that will not waste our time or the customers. At the same time, I want the customer to feel comfortable in our offices. I want them to have a pleasant experience and I want them to want to come back.

Employee Receipt Form

I understand that the information contained in the ...., Inc., Employee Handbook represents guidelines only and that ....
......, Inc., reserves the right to modify this handbook or amend or terminate any policies, procedures, or employee benefit programs at any time, or to require and/or increase contributions toward these benefit programs.

I understand that this handbook is not contract of employment between me and .... Inc. and that I should not view it as such.

I further understand that I am employed on an at-will basis, which means that I may be terminated at any time at the discretion of my employer.

I further understand that no manager or representative of ...., Inc., other than the President, has any authority to enter into any agreement guaranteeing employment for any specified amount of time. I also understand that any such agreement, if made, shall not be enforceable unless it is in writing and signed by both me and the President.

Employee Signature:

_____
Date:_____

Chapter 4   The Staff Structure

Introduction

This chapter will discuss the staff structure that always worked best for us. It was quite narrow with very little management.

Sales People – SP's

The sales staff handled everything from list generation to the marketing materials. They made the phone calls and followed up on the sales calls. If sales needed support they turned to the project managers. The project manager was as far into the organization as the sales people were allowed to go. If necessary the project managers would turn to the writers and developers. Once a salesperson got the contract signed the project manager took over.

Project Managers - PM's

Our project manager's job was very pivotal. First, they supported sales with information for potential customers and making sales calls if necessary. Second, they directly supported their currently assigned projects. This involved coordinating the developers and technical writers in their daily tasks. A third role, which was very important to the company, was their ability to gain constant access to the customers business, moving horizontally across the structure of the customer's organization. In doing so had access to information that could be feed back to the sales department. In turn the sales department would open up other opportunities.

Inherent in the job was also the task of keeping the sales people from distracting the developers. There has never been a sales person that didn't want to ask the developer "just one little question".

Technical Writers – TW's

Technical writers work for the Project Manager. When a signed contract was brought in, to develop a design specification, the PM introduced the TW to the project, the project parameters, and the customer.

The TW then spent the designated time with the customer and the customer's staff developing the specification. At all times the TW reported their progress back to the PM only. The PM in turn monitored and validated the specification. If the TW needed developer support the PM assigned the developer.

A Technical Writer's Job

A Design Specification Definition

> The reason we never became a paperless society was because we're always writing some sort of technical document. With this in mind we created a single, all encompassing, document simply called the "Design Specification".

> The design document stood on it's own with two purposes. The first was to define all aspects of their new software application. All aspects included everything from the reasoning behind the development to user training and implementation. The second purpose is to provide the developers with everything they needed to write the new application, everything from screen layouts to file and query structures. Our expectations were that anyone on the project could pick up a design

specification and know everything was to know about the project, from where our customer had been to where the developers were going.

In addition, once the first two mandates were accomplished successfully, a complete and signed "Design Specification" acted as the platform for all cost estimations, the client / company contract, and a daily working document.

The job of gentle persuasion

As presented earlier, our technical writers worked directly with clients to write the design specification. One aspect, which was very important, was the writer's ability to expand the customer's conceptual view and therefore the size and scope of the design document.

The technical writers' basic working premise was not only to discuss and design the new application, in its strictest parameters, but work with the client to broaden their point of view, making sure they were aware of the technological possibilities.

We made sure that when a customer said they wanted to develop a new piece of software we brought all of our experience to bear on the design process.

The reason we did this was quite often our customers weren't development literate and didn't have exposure to design and development methods. If we had designed the application as the majority of our customers initially perceived it, it would have often been months if not years behind current standards.

Another practice we brought to the writing process was the attempt to persuade the clients not only to design the current application but also to design everything that went with it. We called it "Blue Sky". Our mantra was; It's always more prudent to put in too much than to leave something out.

Why, from the client perspective was Blue Sky prudent?

1. We wouldn't have to rewrite code if we knew future plans. The software would be ready for the future enhancements.

2. A larger design spec could be broken into pieces or phases each with its own cost, thereby spreading out the perceived large price tag.

3. The customer, in a department of a larger organization, has the opportunity to push through expenditures if they're already documented and the cost predetermined or smaller customers the plan could be taken to a bank for planning purposes.

Why, from our perspective was Blue Sky prudent?

1. The more the customer put into the specification the more billable hours we could eventually charge for.

2. The more phases the customer put in the spec the more likely we were to get additional work and more pieces were likely to be done immediately.

3. The more work we received the longer we would maintain the customer.

You need to think about "Blue Skying" the specification like looking at a new car. The more extras a sales person shows you the greater the chance you're going to purchase them. It's difficult to walk away from a GPS system once you've seen it. It's the same with the sale of software development.

[A Story: In the early 90's we built a custom ERP package for a client that originally wanted to spend just over $130,000. I recently went back and added up all the numbers for the original package and all the additions through the years and the total came to nearly $500,000.]

The Developer

It's interesting to note that although the PM is the pivotal person for monitoring and tracking all activities, every real technical detail is built on the skills and expertise of the developers.

In our organization the developers reported to two people. For daily customer work they reported to the project manager. For professional skill support they reported to a manager. The manager made sure they had all the tools they need and were continuing their education or certifications. Our firm's managers lead the process. The PM was the leader of project.

The Project Manager and Technical Writer as part of the Sales Department

No matter how technical these two positions are, you need to select your staff as much for their technical ability as for their abilities to work with the customer and your sales department. These two positions will add tens of thousands of dollars to a single job simply by being aware of and understanding the underlying sales process.

The Operation and Management of a Software Company

Thin Layered Staff Structure

Management Level

Business Level

Sales PM

Technology Level

Technical Writer

Software Developers

Chapter 5 The Cost of Development

Introduction

Calculating the cost of developing a piece of software can be difficult and time consuming. Far too often the calculations are done in your head with a faint hope that you'll have something left over.

Well, this method isn't really doesn't work for more than calculating a day's work, for one person. I've always thought that a lot of business owners never really wanted to figure out the final numbers because if they did, the difference between perception and reality would scare the hell out of them. It doesn't need to.

Taking the time to figure out where those hard-earned dollars are going will make all the difference. You'll know where you stand and what to do next. The sooner you find out the better.

The Cost of Employees

Wages

From the minute you begin the interview till the day the employee leaves, the wages will determine the work you take and therefore the bottom line.

The best way to determine fair pay is to survey wages in your area. Ask other business owners. Take a look at local career boards. The information will give you an idea of where they stand, based on skill sets, for your regional area.

A few words on other business owners, state information and career boards.

When discussing wages with other business owners, be aware of all the extras they may or may not be providing, both tangible and intangible. Then consider what you can or cannot afford.

When reviewing state government information be aware that states generally don't break out, or seemingly account for, the wide range of development skills. I recently reviewed a local state's wage scale. I was looking for average wages for Microsoft VB and C language developers. From what I could tell this particular report rolled all developers into one category, including older languages such as COBOL and RPG. What I finally discovered was that the average wage presented was much lower than the going wage for say Microsoft skills. Each state is a little bit different so be aware.

I think reviewing job boards on the Internet provides the most accurate snapshot of where wages are. I would suggest searching your state or area within the state, keeping in mind the industry that's offering the position. It's a good way to understand what employers are willing to pay and what you're competing against.

One last comment, be careful when reading the trade magazines and annual wages presented. I've always found them to be higher than my own research.

Salary or Hourly

This question is often debated. The determining factor, as to whether you pay hourly or salary, has to be a decision based on whether you're

The Operation and Management of a Software Company

paying a lot of overtime that could be absorbed by paying a salary and the state laws governing when you need to pay salaried overtime.

From an organizational point of view moving from hourly to salary has ramifications, both good and bad.

1. You can project expenses with much more precision.

2. You can get a clearer picture of expenses vs. cash flow.

3. Employees that consistently put in extra hours will see a decrease in wages. Can this decrease be compensated for with other benefits?

4. Your accounting department will put less effort into collecting and calculating payroll.

5. Your project managers will spend less time managing and collecting hours.

I've found employees are more willing to move from hourly to salary than generally thought. It decreases the ups and downs of hourly concerns and provides a more assured and consistent paycheck.

Benefits

Break down benefits into three areas, standard, non-standard, tangible / intangible. Understand benefits are different from company to company and should be considered a framework to start from. Some suggestions are:

1. Standard benefits are health insurance, medical and dental, paid vacation, sick leave, and vacation.

2. Nonstandard benefits are a 401(K), training, personal days, and disability.

3. Tangibles are flex time, free lunches, quarterly company meetings, a lax dress code, a company kitchen, employee committees, employee/family web sites.

4. Intangibles are management style and work environment.

Being an owner, you're aware that each and every benefit provided means less dollars reaching the bottom line. At the very same time you understand that the more benefits you supply the greater the stability your organization. It's a balancing act that only you can deal with.

Let me address some of these benefits:

1. Medical insurance is costly but you can't grow a business without it. When I started the business I couldn't afford insurance. I was lucky though, I found developers that had insurance from other sources. As I grew and began to look for more people it was always the first question. Do I have health insurance? When I could finally answer yes, my pool of potential employees widened. Get medical insurance for your staff as soon as you can afford it.

2. If asking for medical insurance was the first question, training was the second question. Find a

way to train your employees as soon as possible. My method of training was to use Microsoft certifications. I purchased the training material then ask that within a reasonable amount of time those interested would become certified. (It was implied that everyone should be interested.) I paid for the first and second attempt at taking the test. If the employee failed the first two they were expected to continue till they passed. They paid from that point forward. I never had an employee that didn't eventually get their certification.

3. Get a 401(K) in place right away. Even if you can't contribute, it'll make a difference in the hiring process.

4. Flex time is generally easy to provide. Our policy was rather tight but still left room for some flexibility. An employee could start and finish one hour on other side of the standard 8 – 5 work day. In our case it was often important to be there during business hours.

5. Free lunch every other Friday was provided. The opposite Friday was "Bring Your Own Lunch". The time was used to stay close to the staff. We would either cook together in the kitchen or I'd have lunch catered. For the first 15 minutes I would present how the business was doing and ask for questions, and I always got questions. If we had a new employee they would say a few words about themselves and their work history. I would then ask each of our sales and administrative staff to present any issues they might need to discuss. The rest of the time was spent discussing movies, politics and everyone's family. Our lunches had little business and a lot of personal discussion. It made a big difference to

my understanding of our staff and they came to understand me.

6. A semi-lax dress code was put in place. If you've ever been a developer, you'd understand that jeans and sneakers are a lot more comfortable than a tie and wing tips. This is not to say we didn't dress for our clients.

Our policy was that employees must dress to the dress code, dress style, of the clients. It was also requested that everyone have the appropriate clothing in the office at all times, storage was provided. If they didn't know what to wear they were to ask.

7. A company kitchen was put in. It allowed the staff to cook together on Fridays and it was a big plus when the weather got bad. It was a nice addition at little cost.

8. The one employee committee we created, worked very well. It was the developer's committee. Generally speaking all the developers in the company attended if available though they did have a senior representative. Unlike our Friday lunches this meeting was about the development of software only. Discussions ranged from the comfort of the developer to new software and education. I have to say that this one hour every other week kept us moving forward with a minimum of development hitches

9. I've always placed the office in crowded industrial parks near malls or shopping areas. You know the ones, where from Thanksgiving to Christmas

you drive ten feet every ten minutes. Because of location and our busy holiday schedules, came up with a plan that allowed an employee to leave work between the hours of 10am and 2pm to Christmas shop. The stipulation was they had to make up the hours the same day. This was a small concession but it took a lot of stress off the staff.

Vacations

Vacation time varies from company to company but the minimum I would suggest is:

1. New Years Day
2. Memorial Day
3. 4th of July
4. Labor Day
5. Thanksgiving
6. Christmas or Hanukkah

I would also suggest that you consider, at a minimum, a floating holiday to be used for a long weekend.

Training

Training is the most important benefit you can provide next to health insurance. Earlier I explained that I used the MS certification as the method of training our developers. There are a wide variety of other ways, ranging from free programs provided by vendors to week's worth of education in Europe.

Whatever type of training you decide on make sure that the cost of the class is recovered before the employees leaves the company.

Our method for doing so was to prorate the total cost of the class across several months with payment for the full amount of the training due if the employee left the company in less than one year from date of training

Wages and Benefits

In chapter two I discussed hiring the right person for the position. As important as the right skills is the combination of wages and benefits. Working to get these two items balanced takes time and experience.

The cost of all these Employees

To understand the cost of your staff you need to be realistic about what your employees are costing. I would suggest that you determine this number before you do anything else. If you don't know this number you should. Do it on this page with a pencil or use a spreadsheet. Break down the wage, benefits, overhead (the cost of the floor space the person is taking up) and the hours non-billable such as holidays, vacation and training. When you add it up, that's the real cost of doing business, per employee, per hour.

You'll need to take this number even further. Sum up all the employees and then roll in all your non-billable personnel, yourself, the secretary and any others, even if they're on a part time basis. Average this value out and you'll be surprised at how much your cost of doing business really is.

Deal with it now and adjust accordingly. Take a look at what you're charging per hour against what your cost is per hour. Is the difference sufficient for you to do what you

The Operation and Management of a Software Company

want to do? Does this amount get you where you want to go? If it isn't then adjust and do it now.

The Cost of Internal Operations

With all that's said and done in your business nothing takes away from the bottom line faster than losing control of your internal operating costs.

What are Internal Operating Costs? My definition of internal costs is those costs, within your building, that will eat up your margins if not constantly monitored and controlled. The two big ones for software development firms are overhead and billable hours. Get these two broad categories under control, optimize them to the max and you'll do very well. Let either one run out of control and it'll pull you down in a matter of weeks.

Overhead Costs

>Overhead was defined as office space. The other items that normally fall under overhead I believe you know how to control, things like office supplies, electric, heat, etc, but office space is one of the most misspent on items and the one I want to focus on. I'm here to tell you that I didn't get it right as often as I should have.

>[A Story: The first year I ran the business out of a spare bedroom. As the second year rolled around I cleared out the basement and filled it up with developers. It was maybe 300 sq. ft. It filled it up so fast that the driveway couldn't take all the cars. We had to start parking in the church parking lot down the street. By the end of the second year we had to start looking for more room.

Our second office was found above a friend's new dental office. We picked it not for the location but for how many developers we could get in combined with the low per square foot cost. We had never paid rent before and weren't looking forward to it. (Floor space is the first real risk a business owner takes when he starts the business from home. It's not a big deal now but it kept me up at night back then.)

The new office space was two rooms, one big work area and one small conference room. The whole place was about 750 sq. ft. We filled it up with tables and chairs and more employees. Eighteen months later we started looking again.

The next office was extravagant. It was easily 2500 sq. ft., not counting the empty basement. It was carpeted, had a glass walled conference room, offices around the outside and a presence that said we had made it. The decision wasn't just the number of developers we could get in but it's marketing value.

Five years out of the basement and we had arrived. We worked hard to fill it up again. We had twenty-five employees; our clients were Ernst and Young, Microsoft, and The Limited to name a few. Everything we thought had been validated. Validation by the square foot! The only thing that concerned us, through all this success, was that we were in Canton Ohio. We needed to move closer to our larger clients. The closer we got to Cleveland the more serious our clients new and old would take us. Time to move.

The Operation and Management of a Software Company

We went in search of the ultimate office. It had to be within reach of the Cleveland. It had to be cool. We sat down and considered all the earlier mistakes and were ready to adjust. We found just the right place. It was forty miles north of the current office. It was an easy drive to Cleveland, on the far west end of Akron, in Fairlawn Ohio. We designed the layout ourselves It was upscale with dark carpet and walls. The main office space was one big room with IKEA tables and black leather chairs. I put art on the wall and jazz on the stereo. We had arrived again! Our open house brought out a couple hundred clients. We were cool. We were validated with 5000 sq. ft.

We were ready to rock and roll and I was completely wrong.]

[A Story: One thing that drove me to move, though now I believe differently, was that a large multi-national company needed some development work done. We approached the Canton firm but were rebuffed with the explanation there was no company in Canton that could possibly do the sophisticated work they needed done. They were going to look towards Cleveland or Chicago.

The message I heard was "the closer you get to a larger city the more reputable you were"]

In retrospect

In retrospect, when it comes to office space and marketing it I realize I got it wrong. Did we succeed with the way I described? Yes, but we could have done a lot better. We could've been a lot smarter.

It's about square footage stupid!

Our final office was 5000 sq. ft. When we first moved in we only filled up half of the space. We had always grown and there was no reason to think we wouldn't. What I hadn't understood was that overhead is the software firm's basic defense against everything that happens to the company. I just didn't get it. You can't control the economy, developer's lives, or finicky customers but you can control floor space, its cost, and how you put it to use.

Knowing that the staff needs a comfortable work environment, you need to make optimum use of every inch of floor space you're paying for. You need to consider finding ways to optimize your office as precisely as you optimize your servers and workstations. Use less space, double up on shifts, hot swap machines but get the square footage and associated numbers down to where they're reasonable. Less floor space is more when it comes to the bottom line.

What happened to all the visitors?

Art on the wall is wonderful. It makes the employees feel good; it changes the perspective. It makes for a nice place to work but unless you're opening up a gallery or you plan to have dozen clients showing up every week lighten up a little bit. I have to admit that the clients who came through the office were impressed but when I think back on it, we never really had enough customers coming through to make an impact on our bottom line. Did the firm really need this type of presentation to close a software development sale?

From where I stand now, I believe we could have had a nice office for our employees, first, and a presentable office for our customers, second, without going where we went. I'm not convinced that cool and the cost that comes with it sell the final product, at least not in this business.

Location, Location, Location!

I also believe that moving the office closer to my customers was a mistake, for several reasons.

1. The percentage of your clients that actually visit the office is very low. As much as we would like them to visit, like us, they're often far too busy.

2. Moving closer doesn't increase the quality of your work or the numbers of customers pounding down the door. You still need to market and actually, market more, because the cost of the move and associated disruption needs to be paid for.

3. You can't move closer to a prospective client because you don't know who the next prospective client is. Customers are moving targets.

4. Moving closer does not automatically mean you're ever close enough. Software development firms need to define being close as

quality delivery services and not a geographic location.

5. If you spent the same dollars on technology that you spent on moving closer, you'd be as close as the client's conference room with today's satellites, VPN's, and video conferencing.

Think about it this way. Eight billion dollars a year goes offshore to India, 5000 miles away from the US, for $15 to $25 per hour. Customers don't want vicinity they want service.

The bottom line on Office Space

The bottom line is to find the least expensive office space that is comfortable for your staff. Then spend the extra money on other things like communications, salespeople, and marketing.

Billable Hours - the cost of not controlling them

Of all the things we've talked about in this book not controlling billable hours will do most damage fastest. If you only take one thing away from this book it needs to be the importance of <u>managing billable hours.</u> You can do it by understanding and managing your firm's efficiency rate.

What are efficiency rates?

We decided, after moving into our second office, that we needed to have access to the number of hours our developers were billing every day, by the hour. We understood right away these were the numbers that, if we could manage them, would allow us to succeed.

The efficiency rate, as we calculated it, was;

The percentage of hours "actually billed", to the customer, during a particular time period vs. the amount of time "available to bill" the customer, during that same time period.

Time periods begin with a single eight-hour workday and move upward. Billing a customer for 6 hours out of an available 8-hour day is a 75% efficiency rate. What 75% meant to us was that you were losing 25% of your capacity to bill every day.

Development

A Beginning - Internal Efficiency Rates

Begin by tracking the daily hours billable for each individual developer. At the beginning of each week, hand out a paper timesheets, one for each day of the week. Ask the developers to breakdown their day into billable and non-billable using hours and minutes, filling out the sheet as the day goes along.

At the end of each day the billable hours are calculated and moved to the invoice system.

At the same time the efficiency rate should be calculated, asking how many hours were non-billable and why.

The focus must be on non-billable. With the developers' help, work on why you're getting less than 8 hours of billable development work done in an 8-hour day. No one was goofing off. No one was doing anything but coding. Why were you losing 25% of our capacity to bill, per developer, per day? It adds up fast. With 5 developers you can lose 10 hours a day, which is equal to another developer per day plus.

One important aspect of a timesheet is that it allows a snapshot of each of the developer's abilities in completing their work. With this information you can mentor them to keep your efficiency rate on track.

Once you've validated the daily timesheets you can roll them into weekly calculations and from there monthly, quarterly and for the year. Each roll up will give you another perspective on your efficiency rate.

One important thing to consider, when developing a timesheet process, have the developers use the line item numbers, from the initial estimate, as line items on their timesheet. It allows the developers to begin a direct relationship with the customer's project and the particular tasks that make it up

Internal Project Tracking

I would like to start by explaining how we developed our process of internal project tracking.

In the early 90's we used paper. I created a daily timesheet that contained 3 columns. The columns were titled duration, job and description. They were pretty self-explanatory. I collected them at the end of every day, totaled up the billable and non billable hours, entered the billable hours into the accounting system, reviewed them and addressed any development issues the following morning. This was the extent of it. We were too busy to address non-billable or efficiency rates. It was just heads down development and get the bills out on the weekend.

As the jobs grew larger we changed. We added start and stop times to be used for paying wages. We added the designation of billable and no billable to help our administrative person determine what to invoice for. We added a standard nomenclature to the descriptions, to make it easier to understand. It was tough when we had 15 developers each with their own shorthand.

The next change was more significant. Over the first five years of estimating projects we developed a series of spreadsheet calculations that would allow us to complete an estimate in a matter of minutes. In doing so we created very specific line items, line items that were numbered and used in the description area on the timesheet.

The next step was to give each developer on the project estimate spreadsheet, as reference, with the line items on them. Now, as the developers kept their timesheets, the job number and line item number could be used instead of shorthand. With the connection between the estimate and the timesheets made, both the timekeeping and bookkeeping became much more accurate.

Since our accounting dept. now had time on its hands, I asked them to take the billable hours off of the paper timesheets and apply it back to the very same estimating spreadsheet, as actual hours used, per line item. Having written the contract based on the estimate these new numbers would now show us where we were in the delivery process, at the end of each day. The original estimate had a delivery date calculated based on the hours estimated. Now we could calculate a real delivery date. It was great. We allowed everyone to see the spreadsheets, developers and customers alike.

These spreadsheets worked great on a per project basis because they allowed us to track each individual project and its parts. The problem was that as the complexity and number of developers increased it grew tougher to define exactly how each individual developer was doing. The paper work was becoming overwhelming.

The next spreadsheet we created was one that allowed a snapshot view of the individual employee. It had the employee's names down the left side and days of the year across the top, with two columns per day, one billable and the other non-billable. With this spreadsheet we could now calculate individual efficiency rates per day, week, and month without having to go back to the individual timesheets.

The last step was to get rid of the paper and capture the work hours electronically. Having a building full of developers helped. Two parameters were decided on.

1. The first was that the application would be an Internet application. No more carrying around the information or faxing it in.

2. The second parameter was the application would already have all the jobs, job numbers and associated line items in its database. The accounting department would put them in to eliminate mistakes and allow familiarization with A/R.

The final product ended up being a very productive Internet application that everyone made use of, no matter where they were in the country. My only stipulation to our development team was that it be used every night before they went home.

Once the application was in place and working we extended it into managing all the spreadsheets. I have to say that two minutes after the day ended I could finally log on and review absolutely every aspect of the company's efficiency. It made a tremendous difference to our business.

Internal Productivity

From the previous discussions you can tell my focus has always been the efficiency of the staff. Given that the sales force can keep up the supply of work. management's focus needs to be on getting the work done. This type of tracking will have an immediate effect on your business.

Forms: The two following forms are provided.

1. Example of a timesheet
2. Example of a repayment form for training.

Your Company Name   Daily Time Sheet

Day: _Monday_____ Date: __02/12/02_____

Developer Name: _____ Project Name:____
_____

Duration   Billable

From To   Total   Line Item   Y/N   Description

___ ___ _____   _____   ___   _____
_____

___ ___ _____   _____   ___   _____
_____

___ ___ _____   _____   ___   _____
_____

___ ___ _____   _____   ___   _____
_____

Total _____   Billable Hours
Total _____   Nonbillable Hours
       +

Total _____   Hours for the Day

Efficiency Rate For the Day =

_____ / _____
Billable Hours Hours for the Day

Repayment Agreement for Education/Training Expenses

I understand that ...., **Inc.** ("xxx") encourages employees to seek education and/or training to further develop their skills and expertise and that xxx is willing to (1) advance the tuition; (2) reimburse me for out-of-pocket travel expenses; and (3) in some cases, to pay my salary for time spent in class and/or in study. I further acknowledge that xxx undertakes these financial commitments with the understanding that it is making an investment in education that will be used to the future benefit of xxx for at least a reasonable period of time.

I agree that my acceptance of any monies is subject to repayment by me if:

1. I fail to satisfactorily complete the course;

2. I terminate my employment prior to completion of the course; *or*

3. I terminate my employment within twelve (12) months of the completion of the last training class or session.

I agree to repay the amounts owing in full at the time that they become due. I further authorize xxx to deduct and withhold from my final paycheck or paychecks all amounts owing but not to exceed the total amount owed by me. Upon entering into this Agreement, an estimated cost will be calculated. I understand that the actual cost involved, however, will be used to determine the amount owed.

Tuition Cost	$ _____ . 00
Estimated Travel Costs	$ _____ . 00
Estimated Salary During Training/Study	$ _____ . 00

Training Description:

> I have read the above and agree to the terms and conditions therein.

EMPLOYEE:

_____
SIGNATURE

EMPLOYER: ...., Inc.

_____
OFFICER'S SIGNATURE AND TITLE

_____
DATE

Chapter 6. The Cost of Management & Administration

The Efficiency of an In-house Staff

The developers aren't the only ones whose productivity needs tracked.

Project Managers

Project Managers need to be billable as much as possible. When you create the estimate spreadsheet have the PM add their task line items. Put their time against that estimate just like developers. Treat the workload of a project manager the same as any one else's. You may have to adjust their efficiency rate to 50% or 75% but you need to keep track.

Our project managers had several jobs at one time and kept their time across several job numbers and line items.

Accounting / Administration

The accounting department is the center of your company. I would suggest that you make a list of all the things that the accounting and administration people do in a standard time period and put them on an abbreviated spreadsheet. Ask them to put their hours down based on agreed upon line items.

I think you'll get a very interesting picture of where the time goes. From these results you'll want to sit down and figure out how best to optimize what's being accomplished.

[A Comment: I want to say right here that tracking times and hours as billable vs. non-billable, isn't an impediment to your employees. These tasks have one purpose and it is to see that your company operates at its best. Otherwise you're wasting your time. When I first started the business we used to joke that we felt more like a Catholic Charity than a business. So don't]

Clerical / Administration

Again, I would suggest you make a list of the things Clerical / Administrative people do in a standard period of time and put them on an abbreviated spreadsheet.

Understand that doing these spreadsheets for the staff is not only important in optimizing workloads but it goes a long way to showing the staff that you mean business and everyone's time is important.

Management

Management's not going to get out of these considerations. As before, make a list of all the tasks that you do in a month. Use a month's time period, it'll give you a better picture. Then give the tasks a priority rating, say 1 – 5. Put them on an abbreviated spreadsheet and keep track.

One thing that I've always found is that the owner, president, or operations manager of a company tries to do too much and often too much of the wrong thing.

After a week take a look at your spreadsheet. Are you doing the work that falls in the 4 – 5 priority range? Did you do the work you need to do to keep the business going? If you're not, start delegating the 1 – 3 priorities tomorrow. At the end of each week review until your workday is optimize to help the company.

Other Costs to Consider and Control

Rent / Lease

In hindsight, I learned spending a lot on floor space isn't necessary. If you keep in mind the comfort of your staff first and then the esthetics, you'll find more reasonably priced office space.

Utilities

You don't have a lot of control over this one. As you're aware your business is pretty much at the mercy of current prices and the square footage.

One thing that we did to reduce the glare off the monitors and strain on the developer's eyes was to turn down the lights. It did save us a bit of money but not significantly.

Capital Equipment

Hardware

Purchasing a PC for each new developer can be costly but even more costly if they're sitting unused because you have to reduce your staff, lose an employee, or send any employee off site.

One alternative is to create a second shift of developers that uses the same machines and desks used by the first shift. With swappable hard drives this alternative is quite feasible. This method reduces your fixed costs, delivery time, and square footage necessary.

Software

This is a difficult area to get under control. Every company licenses software differently and the visual family of products, whether Oracle, Microsoft or IBM for development purposes are not inexpensive.

I would suggest that before you purchase any product have your developer's committee test it. Decide if a particular product is going to make a difference. A lot of the larger software producers have demo or partner products you can load up and test. One partner program that's worked well over the years is the Microsoft Partner Program. Test it out and then decide what you really need to purchase.

Headhunting phone calls

It's hard to keep hunters away from the employees but there's a way to keep them away once you've found out they're calling. When we got their name (a response to great employee relationships) we did two things, we called and explained they were never to call again and we sent them a bill for time spent on the phone with our employees. They never paid the invoice but they also never called back.

Documentation

Two simple rules; make every document you can a template and don't do any documentation that pertains to a project that's non-billable if you don't have to.

Reading Material

Developers need to keep up on new technologies and there's no way to do it except by reading. Our firm supplied all the books and periodicals our staff asked for. If there was something someone needed they could just ask and we'd order it.

What we did not allow was reading of documentation that was not project oriented, while at work unless we were out of billable or in-house non-billable work. Otherwise they had to take it with them.

Software Storage

Trying to find a piece of software is a big time killer. You can't charge the customer for looking for it, loading it, or waiting for it to be delivered.

The methods we used to handle this were;

1. Select a software librarian to store, catalog, as well as check in and out software needed.

2. Store all the software in a single location

3. Make sure all contract software purchases are ahead of customer needs.

4. Have one person load all the necessary software onto everyone else's machine, preferably on off hours.

Hardware Storage

Just like software, if your machines aren't up to the job, you're going to deal with project slow downs everyday. You can always tell how slow the machines are by how many cups of coffee a developer drinks. And as we all know, software dictates the hardware so don't be afraid to upgrade your machines above and beyond basic software specifications. Ask your developers what they need. They'll tell you.

Backups

If anything can slow you down or even put you out of business it's not doing backups. Our practice was to backup changed work from the workstation to servers twice a day. The servers were backed up every day.

Personnel

Interruptions are another way to lose time. Whether it's from the boss, the administration or just another developer, interruptions can really get in the way of getting things done. Our way of handling it was to use email. Anyone can send anyone else an email, at any time, but the receiving person had the option to set it aside until before lunch or near the end of the day.

Those little personal extras

There are a lot of incidentals that need to get done during the day. If you can make getting these things done easier it'll always benefit productivity in the end. Things like finding a dry cleaner to stop in during the day, a restaurant that delivers, or a valet service that will run errands. Help find ways to meet your employee's needs without distracting from their workday.

Customer meetings

Meetings can really eat up a developer's day. I would suggest the following;

1. If it's a presales or sales meeting and you must use developers make sure that the meeting is well defined and that the developer's time is on the agenda.

2. If it is a presales or sales meeting and you must have a technical meeting attempt to hold the meeting in your office to cut down on travel time.

3. If it's a in-process development meeting the developer's time can be charged for, but make sure that you've accounted for the meetings in the estimate and the contract.

4. If you must hold a meeting with developers and you can't charge for it, create an agenda that calls the developer into the meeting for a specific amount of time. There is no need to have them sit through the preliminaries or wrap up.

Effect on revenue

In the careful tracking and managing of efficiency rates your business has the tools to increase cash flow and generate revenue.

[A Comment: At one point we had ten software developers, all of them in the office on projects. The average billable per day ranged, per developer, at 80% or 6.4 hours per day. We were losing 1.60 hours per day per developer. Across 10 developers we were losing 16 hours per day.

At that time we were charging an average of $80 and we were losing a approximately $1280 per day if we hit a max efficiency of 8 hours. Calculate16 hours across 5 work days and you'll find that we were losing 80 hours per week.

In real billable dollars the loss was $6400 per week. It was a big loss to a little company.

Think about the 80 hours another way. We were losing an equivalent of two developer's billable hours per week. It adds up quick.]

Where does the time go?

So if we were losing 20% a week, with ten developers, where was it going? Everyone was on time, doing their jobs and moving the projects forward.

To find out what's really going on let's break down one developers time for one day and see what happens. Let's find the 1.6 hours we were missing. It's easy to blow 96 minutes in one day. That's only 38 minutes each side of lunch. And don't think of this as a petty consideration, think of it as 20% of your gross revenue disappearing at the end of every day.

Now before anything is said, the list below and the associated discussion aren't trying to be petty or squeeze pennies. What it's trying to do is present where the time and therefore the revenue go and how to make less of an issue of it, personally and professionally.

Coffee

The coffee pot is the life blood of your office. Every developer needs coffee, soda or something to get through the day. I'm the biggest offender. To cut down on time spent to and from and in between consider doing a few simple things.

    1. Get the coffee closer to the developers.

    2. Put the pot out in the middle of the room to discourage long conversations.

    3. Worst case has a non-billable person delivering the coffee and other amenities to the staff.

Lunch

Make it convenient for the employee to get lunch. This isn't to keep anyone away from lunch but make getting it faster, easier, and if possible cheaper. Some suggestions are;

    1. Have a full kitchen, including a refrigerator and stove available.

    2. Put all the carry out menu's together in one place

    3. Get all the menus on-line with the email address of the restaurant.

4. Research restaurants that will give your staff a discount.

5. Provide lunch once a week.

6. Provide a 'bring your own bag lunch' forum around lunch once a week.

Family phone calls

We don't want to stop family calls but pay attention that they don't get out of hand. I'd suggest that if the employee has a real issue at home, that could become distracting; they should use the phone in the conference room for privacy.

[A story: One thing we had to stop a family member from using our 800-phone number to call our employees. When it didn't stop after the first warning we took it out of the next paycheck. It stopped immediately.]

Customer phone calls

Customer calls can be a real killer. It's not the calls for serious issues that are the problem but the ones that call because it's easier than opening the manual, even after training classes.

Customer calls can be broken into two areas, billable and non-billable. Have each developer keep track of daily calls, in 15-minute increments. Place a description next to each and then begin to determine whether they get charged for them.

I'd suggest a customer service contract that addresses phone calls. Make it separate from the development contract.

The bottom line is to get structure to the customer calls. The minutes and hours add up and you may not be able to afford the distractions.

Effect on staff

One thing you can be sure of is everything we have talked about in this chapter will have an effect on your staff. The question is; how will they react to the increased structure? The answer is really up to you and your management staff. You need to present these changes as something that has to done to better control cost, giving everyone involved a healthier company and hopefully the ability to keep those pay raises coming. Presented correctly everyone will understand.

Chapter 7 The Design Specification

Introduction

When you're asked to write a design specification you're going to do it for one of two reasons, to re-engineer a current application or to create something new.

Re-Engineering

I've always enjoyed re-engineering a process or series of processes because I could always see where the client had been as well as where they're going.

The important part of writing a design spec for a re-engineering project is that you need to first review, analyze and capture knowledge of the first or current software application before you can proceed

What I've always done with current applications, if the customer doesn't have the appropriate material, is to do a preliminary analysis, as I would any other piece of software. Then I begin the new design.

A New Software Application

Developing a new application comes with a well-defined set of sequential tasks that allow the technical writer, in cooperation with the customer, to design and document their new software product. Those defined sequential steps are presented in this chapter. Be aware that what I'm presenting can be adjusted and fine-tuned to support the way you do business. Like so much of the information I discuss, use it as a framework to build your own best practices.

Writing the Specification

Remember the final result of this process. I want to repeat what was said about the Design Specification in Chapter 4 "The Design Specification serves two purposes. It provides the customer with a clear picture of the product they want developed and will receive and it provides you with a clear picture of what you're going to build. Once the document is agreed upon, it will provide both parties with the true contractual details of the development project."

The Customer

The customer will use the design specification for several reasons, more business than technical. A few of them are;

>1. To present to management / corporate for funding.

>2. To present to the bank for lending purposes.

>3. To track the development processes.

>4. To use for getting other vendor's estimates.

>5. To use as part of the business / marketing /sales plan

Your Business's Use

Your staff will use the specification for several reasons. A few are;

>1. Estimating the project.

>2. Use as an attachment to the contract

3. Use as a working document for the project manager.

4. Use as a development guide for your developers.

5. Use as a guide for Accounting / Billing Dept.

6. Use as a Sales tool

7. Use as a historical guide for the future

The Structure of the Document

The layout of the design document needs to be in a form that is clear and concise and accomplishes the delivery of the information that's required.

There are two formats presented later in this chapter.

The structure for the customer

Document structure for the customer needs to be considered. As the document is being written the technical writer needs to understand that even though he's writing a very technical blueprint he should allow for a non-technical person to read and understand it.

The structure for your staff

Document structure for the staff needs to be very organized, sequential and understandable. When technical language is necessary it should be used.

I also reminded our technical writers that our customer always have the option to take their design specification to another development firm for comparison and estimate. What do we want the other development firms to say about our work?

Table of Contents

The following pages present two Tables of Contents. The first is simple but works well in collecting the data necessary to meet the parameters set out earlier in this chapter.

The second table of contents is much more complex. This design specification takes into account types of consumers, different development languages, multiple platforms and several different deliverable executables.

The bottom line of each and every specification is its ability to present and provide, very precisely, a project design, a cost estimate, and a timeline.

I'll explain the make up of each. I've always used previously built table of contents as guideline for new ones. Not every specification needs every chapter but as you write more specifications I would suggest creating a template in MS WORD and using a master version to pick and choose.

A Simpler - Table of contents – An explanation

This simple design specification is broken into four areas. This is an example of how a specification is put together. You should adjust it to fit your business.

Section A.)

The first section has two chapters. Chapter 1 is an overview of the complete application, expressed in business terms. The overview allows the customer and your staff to get a good understanding of what's to follow, in non-technical terms. This chapter is the Who, What, When, Where, and Why of the project.

Chapter 2 is a synopsis of the completed document in quantitative technical terms. It presents the reader with all the specifics that can be moved to the estimating process. Though I don't recommend the person estimate the project by only reviewing these pages it is possible to do so without reading the document.

Section B.)

Chapter 3 is a graphic representation of the data as it flows through the applications, associated screens, databases and reports. This chapter is important to give both technical and non-technical people a view of how the data is expected to move. It's quite acceptable, as complexities grow, to create two of these, one for each type of reader.

Chapter 4 is a written description of the graphic representation to allow for discussion of the process. This area is again written in both business and technical terms to make sure there are no misunderstandings or miscommunications.

Section C.)

Chapters 5 and 6 present the reader with all of the menus layouts, graphically, and a description of the pull downs function, text, colors, etc.

Chapters 7 and 8 present the readers with all of the screen layouts, graphically, and a description of all fields, titles, text, buttons, colors, etc.

Chapter 9 presents the readers with all of the maintenance screen layouts, graphically, and a description of all fields, titles, text, buttons, colors, etc. Maintenance screens were broken out here to allow them to be estimated separately.

Chapters 10 and 11 present the reader with all of the report layouts, graphically, and a description of all fields, titles, and text.

Chapter 12 presents the reader with all of the screen and report query layouts.

Chapter 13 presents the readers with all of the databases, table, fields, field names, and definitions.

Note: Chapters 5 through 13 are the areas that the developers will turn to, to complete their work. I've always reminded our technical writers that the more complete the chapters are the less the developers will ask questions. The less the developer has to search for information, the better job the technical writer has done.

Section D.)

Chapter 14 presents the reader with how security is going to be handled internally and externally. If there are maintenance screens and databases they are discussed but the actual screens and / or tables should be presented in Section C.

Chapter 15 presents the reader with how administration of the databases is going to be handled. The actual screens and tables that actually accomplish the administration should be presented in Section C.

Chapter 16 discusses the integration of information from the application to other associated applications. This area can have a large impact on the estimate and should be written as complete and detailed as possible.

Chapter 17 discusses how project management will handle the development process. I would suggest that the customer's side of the project responsibilities be included.

Chapter 18 presents how meetings will be handled and where located. This area addresses regular meetings as well as how to handle those out of scope.

Chapter 19 presents the customer and the staff with the work that needs to be accomplished before the project can begin and lays out the responsibility of each party.

Chapter 20 presents the testing plan and lays out the responsibility of each party. Responsibilities are very important. If the customer is to participate then detail when and how.

Chapter 21 presents the implementation plan and lays out the responsibility of each party. Make sure that the customer's systems configurations are presented here to allow the development team an understanding.

Chapter 22 presents the training plan and lays out how it is to be accomplished. Be very detailed.

Chapter 23 presents the reader with a discussion of additional phases whether included in the specification or not. This chapter is to prepare the client and the developers for future work.

Chapter 24 presents the project and development team. This chapter should include phone numbers, pagers, and any other information pertinent to the completion of the project.

Chapter 25 presents the readers with "Other Considerations". This chapter is any subject that is of concern to the project that may not fit into a specific category.

Chapter 26 is simply all of the contact information for both your organization and the customers.

Chapter 27 is the Development Estimate. Attach you final project estimate to the design specification

Chapter 28 is the Development Contract.

If at all possible attach the development contract to the specification. Make it easy as possible for your customer to sign.

A Simpler - Table of contents

Sectional Index

Section No.	Description	Page No.
1. The Application		
	1. Application Overview	2
	2. Application Components	4
2. The Flow		
	3. Project Data Flow	6
	4. Data Flow Description	8
3. The Specific's		
	5. Menu Description	10
	6. Menu Layout	12
	7. Screen Description	14
	8. Screen Layout	16
	9. Maintenance Screens	18
	10. Report Description	20
	11. Report Layout	22
	12. Screen / Report Query Layout	24
	13, Table Description	26

4. The Details

14.	Security	28
15.	Administration	30
16.	Connecting to Other Applications	32
17.	Project Management	34
18.	Meetings	36
19.	Up front work to be completed	38
20.	Testing	40
21.	Implementation	42
22.	Training	44
23.	Additional Phases	46
24.	Software Developers	48
25.	Other Considerations	50
26.	Contact	52
27.	The Estimate	54
28.	The Development Contract	56

The Operation and Management of a Software Company

A Complex - Table of contents and explanation

This design specification is broken into seven areas. The reason was the customer not only wanted a stand-alone consumer product in Windows but also wanted a standalone MAC version, an ASP version, and a web site for marketing purposes.

I will present the chapters that were not discussed in the simpler version

Section A.)

Chapters 1 – 7 presents a complete project overview of details involved in developing an application that has more than one platform and can be up and down loaded from the stand-alone. What's important here is to do your research and present the complexities of what needs to be accomplished.

Chapter 1 discusses the consumer and how they will use the software application.

Chapter 2 discusses operating systems across not only various Window's platforms but across MAC's, Unix, and AS400's.

Chapter 3 discusses the options for one language across multiple platforms.

Chapter 4 discusses the feasibility of loading of databases between various platforms and a web site.

Chapter 6 discusses public domain issues per the consumer and the customer.

Section B.)

Chapter 2 is an in-depth discussion of how best to develop an application that would run across multiple window OS's and browsers.

Chapter 5 is a discussion of the artwork and graphics that would be on the screen and therefore seen at all times by the consumer.

Chapter 13 presents the third party products to be used. This chapter made the customer aware that these would be separate charges beyond the hourly rate.

Section C-1)

It is a brief discussion as to the MAC standalone application.

Section C-2)

An in-depth discussion as to the ASP application.

Section D.)

Chapter 3 presents the use of credit card processing for the purpose of purchasing additional add-on items to the stand-alone application, e-commerce portion of the web site.

Section F.)

Chapter 6 presents a complete synopsis of all the components to be developed.

Chapter 7 presents the customer with the cost of the development

Chapter 8 presents the customer will the timeline to complete the development

Please note that even though the second project is several times larger in size than the first, a majority of the chapters of the document are the same. This consistency is important both in standardizing the content and in estimating the project.

Be aware that the design document can be used an attachment to the legal services contract and should be written as such, even if it isn't eventually used. You can see from Section F., Chapters 7 – 8, we did intend to use this document as such.

Also, per previous discussions, the use of the template method for creating the design specification is a good method for keeping your firm's documents consistent. And consistency is important in estimating, service contracts, developing the software and historical analysis.

Keep in mind that the specification template is a living tool that should have any new Section or Chapter added to it.

Once added your technical writer should, with the support of project manager, determine whether a paragraph is used or not.

A more complex Table of Contents

Sectional Index

Section No.	Description	Page No.
Chapter No.		
Important Note		2
Glossary		4
Section A.	Project Overview	6
Chapter 1	Consumer Use Diagram	8
Chapter 2	Operating Systems	10
Chapter 3	Languages Options	12
Chapter 4	Databases	14
Chapter 5	File Flow Diagram	16
Chapter 6	Public Domain Library Discussion	18
Chapter 7	Independent Software Applications Diagram	20
Appendix		22
Section B.	Windows Stand Alone	24
Chapter 1	Software Application	26
Chapter 2	Software Application Platforms	28

Chapter 3	Application Components	30
Chapter 4	Menu Description/Layout	32
Chapter 5	Above the Task Bar	34
Chapter 6	Task Bar Buttons/Layout	36
Chapter 7	Vertical Buttons/Layout	38
Chapter 8	Screen Description/Layout	40
Chapter 9	Screen Query Description/Layout	42
Chapter 10	Report Description/Layout	44
Chapter 11	Report Query Layout	46
Chapter 12	Table Layout/Description	48
Chapter 13	Third Party Products	50
Chapter 14	Security	52
Chapter 15	Test and Implementation	54
Appendix		56
Section C-1.	MAC Standalone Software Application	58
Section C-2.	On-line Web - Software Application	60
Section D	The Web Site	60

Chapter 1	Software Application		60
Chapter 2	Software Application Platforms		62
Chapter 3	Credit Card Processing		64
Chapter 4	Components		66
Chapter 5	Vertical Buttons/Layout		68
Chapter 6	Screen Description/Layout		70
Chapter 7	Screen Query Layout		72
Chapter 8	Report Description/Layout		74
Chapter 9	Report Query Layout		76
Chapter 10	Table Layout/Description		78
Chapter 11	Third Party Products		80
Chapter 12	Security		82
Chapter 13	Test and Implementation		84
Section E.	Web Site Administrative		86
Chapter 1	Application Components		88
Chapter 2	Vertical Buttons/Layout		90
Chapter 3	Page Description/Layout		92
Chapter 4	Screen Query Layout		94

Chapter 5	Report Description/Layout	96
Chapter 6	Report Query Layout	98
Chapter 7	Table Layout/Description	100
Chapter 8	Third Party Products	102
Chapter 9	Security	104
Chapter 10	Implementation Testing	106
Section F.	The Business of Development	
Chapter 1	Meetings	108
Chapter 2	Project Management	110
Chapter 3	Training	112
Chapter 4	Development Methodology	114
Chapter 5	Standard Communication	116
Chapter 6	Design Doc Component Synopsis	118
Chapter 7	Estimated Project Costs	120
Chapter 8	Estimated Project Timeline	122

The Purpose of a Design Specification

The next several pages is a document that was written for the purpose of discussing the design document. It details why the customer needs to have one written before they attempt the development of an application AND why we can't tell them what it's going to cost until the document is completed.

The writing of a Software Design Specification serves three purposes:

1. It provides <u>the customer</u> with a clear picture of the product they want developed and will be delivered by the developer.

2. It provides <u>the developer</u> with a clear picture of software application to be built for the customer.

3. It provides <u>both parties</u> with the true contractual details for the development the product."

The analogy of a design specification and a house blueprint is quite a strong one. You can't reasonably ask someone to build you a house without a blueprint, and you can't create a blueprint without knowing how much you have to spend.

Now, it has to be said that, yes, you can build a house without a blueprint or setting cost expectations but it's a disaster looking to happen.

The advantages, to the customer, in writing a Software Design Specification:

1. To allow for a clear picture, or blueprint, of the application to be built.

2. To allow for a well reasoned cost estimate of the application.

3. To allow for a well reasoned time line for development.

4. To allow for the possibility of a bidding process.

5. To present to management / corporate for funding.

6. To present to a financial institution for lending purposes.

7. To allow for project tracking during the development processes.

8. To allow for a well defined contractual agreement.

The advantages, to the developer, in writing a Software Design Specification:

1. To allow for a clear picture, or blueprint, of the application to be built.

2. To allow for a well reasoned cost estimate of the application.

3. To allow for a well reasoned time line for development.

4. To use as a working document for the project manager, during the development processes.

5. To use as a working document for the developers, during the development processes.

6. To allow for a well defined contractual agreement.

7. To use as a guide for accounting / billing department.

8. To use as a sales tool and historical guide.

Business justifications for a specification before an estimate;

1. The specification is the customer's intellectual and business property.

2. The specification will present the full picture, a qualified perspective, of what is to be developed, before it is developed.

3. The specification will allow for an exact cost of the development to be undertaken.

4. The specification can be used as an attachment to the contract and therefore disallows the need for time and materials contract.

5. The specification will allow for a bid process to be undertaken.

Do you give rough estimates?

Ok, lets say the customer wants a rough estimate, before the spec, after one simple meeting, what are the risks?

1. Incorrect expectations are set – even when explained that estimate is rough.

2. If the final cost doesn't match the earlier rough estimate the client has opportunity to complain, be dissatisfied, or both and rightfully so.

3. An incorrect budget, loan, and expenses can be set based on a rough estimate.

4. The incorrect tendency is to adjust the specification to meet the incorrect rough estimate thereby possibly giving the customer something different than asked for.

5. Giving a rough ballpark estimate allows the customer to make a judgement, as whether to proceed, completely based on an incorrect number.

Chapter 8   Estimating the Design Specification

Introduction

The connection between the design specification and the estimate are those chapters of the completed specification that will cause your firm to generate billable hours. Those specific items, these specific tasks, need to be moved to a project estimate on a line-by-line basis.

The majority of the information needed to create an estimate should have been place in the Applications Components / Synopsis portion of the specification.

Tools to Use

There are a lot ways to create a project estimate, from pencil and paper to software, but the easiest and safest way is to use a spreadsheet. The reason I prefer this method is that I can constantly check and double-check the underlying calculations. This is important because once the final numbers are calculated there's no going back on them. A simple error can mean working for months down the road... free of charge.

Creating a Simple Estimating Spreadsheet

The spreadsheet is quite simple.

1. Down the left hand side, in the second column, enter in the information from the specification. Enter in each menu name, screen name, report name, screen and report query names, and table/database that needs building as well as testing, documentation, setup, etc.

    These are the items your staff works on "every" day.

2. In the first column, number the line items sequentially. The developers can use these line item numbers when applying their daily billable hours.

3. The third column is for quantity of each item in column two.

4. The Fourth column is used to enter the number of hours it will take to accomplish one line item task.

5. In the Fifth column enter in the total hours or quantity times hours per one. If you would have 2 in the quantity and 2 hours each the total would be 4 hours.

6. In column six, Actual Hours, goes the number of hour billed on each item from the developer's timesheet.

7. In column seven put the dollar per hour value for that specific job.

8. In column eight multiple the total number of hours times the dollar per hour number giving you a cost to charge the client for that specific line item.

The Operation and Management of a Software Company

9. At the bottom of Column 5 and 8 sum them up. These numbers will tell you the total number of hours and total cost of the project.

10. Directly under the total hours you'll need to place another number, total number of days. Make sure that you divide the total hours by the real efficiency rate, or billable hours per day, to come up with the real number of days to complete.

11. Under "Days" calculate total weeks to complete.

12. The next part of the spreadsheet are items that are worked on for "part of each week".

13. In column two enter in items such as project management, business meetings, training and / or any other item that's part of the project but not necessarily development work.

14. In the third column enter in a calculation of the number of weeks * the number of hours per week. For example the PM will take 8 hours per week for a 10-week project or 80 hours. Do the same for the other line items.

15. Fill in the cost per hour for your PM and / or testers, etc.

16. Sum up the hourly and weekly costs for a grand total

17. Add in the days and weeks for the complete project.

A review of the spreadsheet

If you take a look at the completed spreadsheet you can see that absolutely all the necessary tasks are presented. The most difficult part of creating this spreadsheet is giving each line item an individual number of hours to complete. Doing this involves working with a developer to come up with a valid number of hours.

A second type of spreadsheet

A second type of spreadsheet can be seen in example. Instead of breaking down each menu, screen, report etc. into separate line items they can be broken down in to low medium and high difficulty. It is more time consuming to group them but once you do, you can use a standard number vs. a unique number in the previous spreadsheet.

The Pros and Cons

The first spreadsheet is more precise but you'll need a developer to calculate the line items each time. The second spreadsheet requires a developer to group them but you can apply standard numbers just faster.

The second spreadsheet is less accurate when it comes to analyzing historical data. If you use the first sheet you can track exactly where you went right or wrong months down the road.

I would recommend you use the first one. The reason is your developers should be supplying you, at the end of each day, with line item numbers and spent hours. When the numbers are applied to this spreadsheet you can see the progress your staff is making with much more precision and that's what this business is all about.

The Completed Estimate

In the simplest terms, the spreadsheet estimate can be used to calculate the hours and dollars, which can be moved directly to the contract.

There are other functions I suggest using it for. They are:

1. Use it as an attachment to the contract.

2. Use it prior to a project to determine manpower needs.

3. Add a column that accounts for actual hours spent billable on each line item.

4. Sum up the actual billable hours spent and calculate an adjusted end date.

5. Use the actual hours spent to track performance daily

6. Place all or part of the spreadsheet on a secure Internet site that the customer can review at regular intervals.

7. Add a calculation to calculate efficiency rates.

8. Use as a part of the project wrap up.

Understand that the spreadsheet is a tool to be used to fit your business objectives. Add or subtract the numbers and / or calculations you need to get the job done but do use something to help you determine scale and cost. A spreadsheet is a good cheap method to do so.

Think about it this way. A spreadsheet tells you;

    A.   Where you're going - before you do the project.

    B.   Where you are - during the project.

    C.   Where you've been once it's complete.

The Operation and Management of a Software Company

Spreadsheet # 1

	A	B	C	D	E	F	G	H
1								
2	Project: Big 5 Client							
3								
4		Task to be		Hours	Total	Actual	Fee per	
5	Task #	Completed	Qnty	Per Qty	Hours	Hours Spent	Hour	Cost
6								
7	1	Menu Bar	3	2	6		$75.00	$450.00
8	2	Vertical Button	13	2	26		$75.00	$1,950.00
9	3	Task Bars	9	2	18		$75.00	$1,350.00
10								
11	4	Screen - low	0	2	0		$75.00	$0.00
12	5	Screen - medium	24	4	96		$75.00	$7,200.00
13	6	Screen - High	0	8	0		$75.00	$0.00
14								
15	7	Screen Queries - low	0	2	0		$75.00	$0.00
16	8	Screen Queries - medium	11	4	44		$75.00	$3,300.00
17	9	Screen Queries - high	0	6	0		$75.00	$0.00
18								
19	10	Reports - low	0	1	0		$75.00	$0.00
20	11	Reports - medium	12	4	48		$75.00	$3,600.00
21	12	Reports - high	0	8	0		$75.00	$0.00
22								
23	13	Report Queries - low	0	2	0		$75.00	$0.00
24	14	Report Queries - medium	7	4	28		$75.00	$2,100.00
25	15	Report Queries - high	0	8	0		$75.00	$0.00
26								
27	16	Screen reports - low	0	4	0		$75.00	$0.00
28	17	Screen reports - medium	12	6	72		$75.00	$5,400.00
29	18	Screen reports - high	0	12	0		$75.00	$0.00
30								
31	19	Screen Report Queries - low	0	1	0		$75.00	$0.00
32	20	Screen Report Queries - medium	0	2	0		$75.00	$0.00
33	21	Screen Report Queries - high	0	3	0		$75.00	$0.00
34								
35	22	Tables	17	4	68		$75.00	$5,100.00
36								
37	23	Security	0	16	0		$75.00	$0.00
38								
39	24	Testing	1	0.5	0.5		$75.00	$37.50
40								
41	25	Doc - Technical Manual	1	24	24		$75.00	$1,800.00
42								
43	26	Training	1	20	20		$75.00	$1,500.00
44	27	License Copies of	0	20	0		$75.00	$0.00
45	27	Third Party Items	4	20	80		$75.00	$6,000.00
46	29	Set - SQL	0	16	0		$75.00	$0.00
47								
48					========	========		================
49				Total Numbers	530.5	0		$39,787.50
50				Toal Days	66.31			
51				Total Weeks	13.26			

Spreadsheet # 2

	A	B	C	D	E	F	G	H	I
1									
2	Project: Big 5 Client				(Complete Spreadsheet)				
3									
4		Task to be		Hours	Total	Actual	Fee per		
5	Task #	Completed	Qnty	Per Qty	Hours	Hours Spent	Hour	Cost	
6									
7		Menu Bar							
8	1	Pull Down A	1	2	2		$75.00	$150.00	
9	2	Pull Down B	1	3	3		$75.00	$225.00	
10	3	Pull Down C	1	6	6		$75.00	$450.00	
11									
12		Vertical Button - 13 buttons							
13	4	Buttons 1-3	3	1	3		$75.00	$225.00	
14	5	Buttons 4-12	8	2	16		$75.00	$1,200.00	
15	6	Buttons 13	1	4	4		$75.00	$300.00	
16									
17	7	Task Bars	1	8	8		$75.00	$600.00	
18									
19	8	Log-In Screen	1	2	2		$75.00	$150.00	
20	9	Screen #2	1	9	9		$75.00	$675.00	
21	10	Screen #3	1	4	4		$75.00	$300.00	
22	11	Screen #4	1	8	8		$75.00	$600.00	
23	12	Screen #5	1	12	12		$75.00	$900.00	
24	13	Screen #6	1	16	16		$75.00	$1,200.00	
25									
26	14	Screen 1 Query #1	1	2	2		$75.00	$150.00	
27	15	Screen 2 Query #1	1	4	4		$75.00	$300.00	
28	16	Screen 2 Query #2	1	4	4		$75.00	$300.00	
29	17	Screen 3 Query #1	1	4	4		$75.00	$300.00	
30									
31	18	Report - Balance Sheet	1	8	8		$75.00	$600.00	
32	19	Report - User Login	1	8	8		$75.00	$600.00	
33	20	Report - Setup Slip	1	8	8		$75.00	$600.00	
34	21	Report - Prep	1	8	8		$75.00	$600.00	
35	22	Report - Inventory	1	6	6		$75.00	$450.00	
36	23	Report - Acct's Payable	1	6	6		$75.00	$450.00	
37									
38	24	Report Query - Balance Sheet	1	4	4		$75.00	$300.00	
39	25	Report Query - User Login	1	6	6		$75.00	$450.00	
40	26	Report Query - Setup Slip	1	6	6		$75.00	$450.00	
41	27	Report Query - Prep	1	8	8		$75.00	$600.00	
42	28	Report Query - Inventory	1	2	2		$75.00	$150.00	
43	29	Report Query - Acct's Payable	1	2	2		$75.00	$150.00	
44									
45	30	Screen Reports - Payables	1	4	4		$75.00	$300.00	
46	31	Screen Reports - Inventory	1	4	4		$75.00	$300.00	
47	32	Screen Reports - Balance Sheet	1	4	4		$75.00	$300.00	
48									
49	33	Screen Report Queries - Payables	1	1	1		$75.00	$75.00	
50	34	Screen Report Queries - Inventory	1	1	1		$75.00	$75.00	
51	35	Screen Report Queries - Balance Sheet	1	1	1		$75.00	$75.00	
52									
53									
54	36	Inventory Table	1	4	4		$75.00	$300.00	
55	37	Login Table	1	4	4		$75.00	$300.00	
56	38	Acct. Balance Table	1	4	4		$75.00	$300.00	
57									
58	39	User Security	1	24	24		$75.00	$1,800.00	
59									
60	40	Application Testing	1	24	24		$75.00	$1,800.00	
61									
62	41	Doc - Technical Manual - Admin	1	40	40		$75.00	$3,000.00	
63	42	Doc - Technical Manual - User	1	24	24		$75.00	$1,800.00	
64									
65		Training							
66	43	Training	1	24	24		$75.00	$1,800.00	
66	44	Set - SQL	1	16	16		$75.00	$1,200.00	
67									
68					=======	=======		============	
69				Total Numbers	358	0		$26,850.00	
70				Toal Days	44.75				
71				Total Weeks	8.95				
72									
73									
74	45	Project Management	8.95	1	8.95	0	$75.00	$671.25	
75	46	Training Meetings	11.45	2	22.9	0	$75.00	$1,717.50	
76	47	Business Meetings	8.95	2	17.9	0	$75.00	$1,342.50	
77					=======	=======		============	
78				Total Numbers	407.75	0		$30,581.25	
79				Toal Days	50.97				
80				Total Weeks	10.19				

Chapter 9   Developing the Application

Introduction

Now this is where the orchestra starts to play. Until now it's been single instruments playing alone. You've had a sales person get the spec contract signed, the technical writer has created a design document, the sales person has come back again with the development contract signed. The solo acts have been completed. Now it's time for the orchestra.

By this Time

By this time you should have several things accomplished. They are;

1. The Project Manager is selected and ready to go

2. The team of developers are selected and scheduled.

3. The PM should have the project book started with all materials from sales notes to copy of signed spec contract in it.

4. The PM should have the role and tasks of each developer.

5. A copy of the design specification handed out to the developers.

6. The developers should be informed of the line items that are assigned, per the design spec. and estimate.

7. A kick off meeting should be scheduled with all parties involved.

8. The correct software for the job should be loaded on all team machines.

9. All hardware should be validated for compliance to the project

10. The back up plan should be distributed to all team members

11. A team member should be assigned to assure back ups are being done.

12. Hard drive and folder structure should be set aside and the information distributed to all team members.

13. A standard time sheet reporting method distributed to all team members.

14. All developers should know what is expected on their Daily Notes.

15. Set aside email addresses for the customer.

16. If feasible supply the customer with login to your servers for review purpose.

The Project Manger

The PM gets the project started. He knows the schedules of all the team members and can, over a specified period of time, have the developers begin, based on their current workload.

I'd also suggest that as the project gets ramped up management personnel take a direct interested in how things are moving forward.

The Developers

As the project begins to pick up speed make sure that every member of the team is on a level playing field. Make sure that everyone uses the time sheet application and keeps good daily notes. Make sure that junior members of the team are up on servers, back ups and file structure. It's suggested that each team have a senior lead developer that has the ability to lead. See that you supply the developers with blank change and issue orders.

The Technical Writer

Though the tech writers job is to complete a spec and start on another project, they should be kept informed that the project is active and should make themselves available for questions.

The Customer

The most important thing a project manager must do is keep the customer informed. However you do it, make sure it's always done on schedule and that each meeting or review is fully documented.

Accounting

One of the biggest pitfalls of a project is not keeping the billing dept. / accounting informed. It starts with making sure they see each and every contract and change order. The assigned PM should be responsible for building and maintaining a relationship with the assigned accounting person. This assures all invoices go out on time, payments are made on time, and that the PM knows, from accounting, when there are collection issues. You may want to consider having the accounting person attend regular in-house project meetings.

Keeping it All on Track

As the project begins, its management's job to review time sheets, spreadsheets and invoices.

Time Sheets

Make sure that the predetermined efficiency rates are being hit. If they aren't, address the issue the first thing each morning. If you don't it'll be difficult to make up the lost time and you can't afford to have this issue get out of hand.

Estimate Spreadsheet

Make sure that the numbers that are coming in from the developers to single line items on the spreadsheets are within your expectation. If they aren't, start asking questions.

Billing

Make sure that the invoices are going out and that the checks are coming in and not the other way around. Review the terms of the contract. If they aren't being adhered to, get on the phone.

The Bottom Line

The bottom line, no matter how many tools you have, no matter how smart your guys are, you have to stay on top of each and every project. Check the numbers make them balance, and then go on. The most important position in your company is the one that makes sure these numbers are where they're suppose to be.

Chapter 10   The Project Book

The Project Book

In discussing the process of writing contracts, developing and writing specifications, writing more contracts, and developing the application there needs to be a central "living" repository for all of the information. That's the job of the Project Book.

A project book should start the minute you write the first set of meeting notes. If you don't get work from the customer the documents can be filed away, but if the relationship grows and moves forward you will need a single, immediate, central location for all the information, both yours and the customers. Use a wide 3 ring binder with the client name and project name on the outside.

Birth – The Sales Dept

The sales department starts the binder. Meeting notes, research on the customer and the project go in the front. When the sales department writes the first contract for the design specification a copy of it goes in. When the customer signs the contract a signed copy replaces the unsigned. (Store the originals in accounting.)

When the technical writer has completed the design spec put it and "all" associated notes in the binder. Place it under a tab named Original Spec. This process is time consuming but it's worth every minute when problems arise.

The next items to go in are the sales department documents per getting the customer to sign the development contract. Again this includes all addendums, changes, adjustments to the design specification and contracts. When the development contract is signed a copy goes in the binder.

Life – The Project Manager

Once the development contract is signed the binder is passed to the project manager. Though copies of the specifications are handed out to the development team the official one remains in the binder.

The PM begins by adding their notes, as the project progresses, including all notes between them, the client, and developers.

Any changes that occur to specification during the development process, made via change orders and their resolutions, are filed. Issue orders also go in the binder with their resolutions.

Testing results at various milestones and predetermine sign offs of both staff and client are filed.

Time sheets or time sheet reports can be filed if deemed necessary. I'd suggest a separate binder.

It's important during the growth and adjustments to the project book that one person be responsible for its well-being. Though the development team must have access, make sure that only one person adds and subtracts information. Generally speaking the best person is the project manager.

Once the project nears its end there will be a series of sign offs that you should request from the client, including the warranty document. Copies of the sign off's must be filed.

Once the project implementation is underway the Sales Dept. should be notified and the project book should be made available for their review.

The project book should remain with the project manager during the warranty period.

Once the warranty is complete the project manager should collect the developer's Daily Project Notes file them in the book, put a big old rubber band around the monster and hand it back to the sales department.

Retirement – The Sales Dept

Once a project is completed, or near the end, the sales department has a responsibility to address a continuing relationship with the customer as well as add another successful project to the company literature. Therefore I would suggest that the final binders, at the very least, reside with the sales dept.

One thing you may want to consider is to deliver a copy of the completed binder, full of notes and history, to the customer.

134   Chapter 10: The Project Book

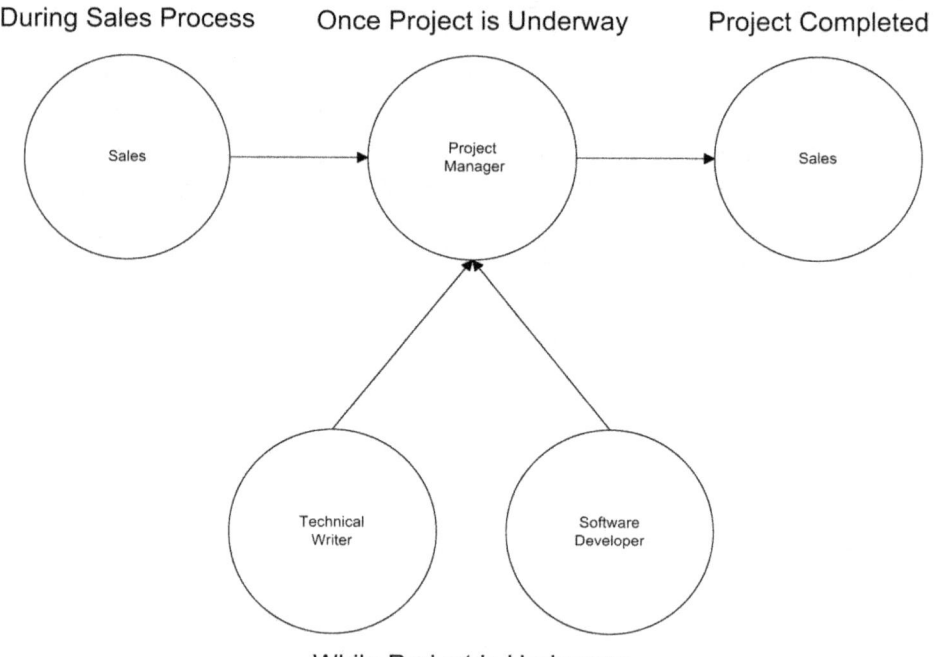

The Operation and Management of a Software Company

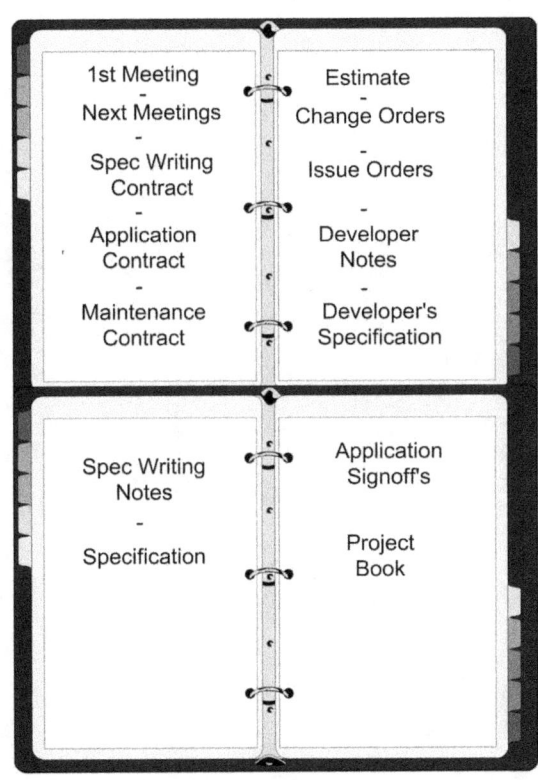

Chapter 11   Change and Issue Orders

Introduction - Change and Issue Orders

Change and Issue Orders help keep control of a project by presenting any additions, changes, or deletions the customer or your staff may find necessary, in an orderly fashion. They're important to the life of the project.

Change Orders

The Change Order is a formal document that should be handed to the customer along with the initial design spec contract. It should be explained that if they wish to change anything, in the design spec, once the contract has been signed, an order is to be filled out and passed to the Project Manager.

Once the PM has received the document it should be passed to the person that originally estimated the project and asked to calculate new hours as well as address any other adjustments that are necessary based on the requested change. The changes and associated hours should be put on the Change Order, signed by the developer, the PM and sent back to the customer for a signature.

I can't stress this enough. <u>Do not make the changes to the application until the customer signs the document and returns it to you</u>! Then and only then, pass a copy to the developer, add it to the project book, pass the original to accounting and make it an addendum to the contract. Then make the code changes.

Issue Orders

Issue Orders are standard documents that address anything that is not a change to the design specification, from the behavior of an individual developer to changing a meeting location.

The importance of this document is in the discussion it creates as to the effect the issue has on the project and what should be done about it. Some issues are moved to Change Orders and some are handled without.

Your Company Name   Change Order Form

Date:_____

Request Made By: _____

Change(s) to be Made:

_____
_____
_____
_____
_____
_____
_____
_____
_____
_____
_____
_____
_____
_____
_____
_____

Note: Add additional information to this document as needed.

Change Order Form Continued

For "Your Company Name" Use Only --------------

Person(s) Responding: _____
_____

Action Taken: _____

Hours +/-: _____   Cost +/-: _____

Action Date: _____

Project Manager Signature: _____
_____

Date: _____

Developer Signature: _____
_____

Date: _____

Note: Add additional information to this document as needed.

Your Company Name   Issue Form

Date: _____

Request Made By: _____

Issue:

_____
_____
_____
_____
_____
_____
_____
_____
_____
_____
_____
_____
_____
_____

For "Your Company Name" Use Only --------------

Person(s) Responding: _____

Action Taken: _____

Action Date: _____

Project Manager Signature: _____

Date: _____

Management Signature: _____

Date: _____

Note: Add additional information to this document as needed.

Chapter 12   Daily Developer Notes

Daily Developer Notes

Though your developers will fill out daily time sheets it's important that they keep another set of notes and those are call the "Daily Developer Notes"

The Daily is generally a spreadsheet or word document that is always up on the desktop and available to the developer to write down random notes as the day progresses. A spreadsheet works better because you can have a standard format for all staff members.

The main purpose this document is a legal one, though it can serve several others. When a client calls a developer and says "make a little change" and later doesn't recall it but their invoice is higher and they've changed their minds, take it out and now the billable is even higher and the application doesn't match the spec and I'm not paying for it and, and, and.

It's easier to take simple notes of phone calls, conversations, suggestion, etc. and pass them to the project manager than to end up with a disaster on your hands.

The other immediate benefit to the developers, even though they have to take a few minutes out, is that once it's written down they can pass it off to the PM and won't have to be concerned until the PM brings it back as change or issue order. The daily document actually allows the developer to focus on the work in front of them and not get caught up in the other activities.

Make sure the Daily Notes go into the Project Book.

Chapter 13   Invoicing for Services Rendered

Invoicing

The software development business is 100% labor intensive. There's just no way around it. And being so, the business's cash flow will always be a recurring issue and an issue that always seems to need immediate attention. Let's discuss several areas of invoicing.

Terms

Terms - the shorter the better and not just for cash flow issues. The shorter the terms the more control you have over other things that can happen. If a client, for whatever reason slows or stops payment you have the ability to stop the development process sooner, decreasing the damage.

Think about it this way, if you have terms of 45 days, then you're going to invest 45 days of development multiplied by the number of developers before you can start to put on the brakes. The damage is already done. Two developers at 45 days at $80.00 an hour is $57,600.00 you're putting at risk.

You may need to consider shortening the terms and keep shortening them until the particular customer yells stop. If you can't get them down where you want, you may want to consider adjusting the hourly rate to make up the difference. Make sure that your contracts take into account late payments.

There's another consideration and that is stopped work. The shorter the payment terms the more discussions you can afford with the customer before you stop work. At 45 days you really can't keep working, but at 15 days you can afford to wait for the return call. If you do decide to stop work it comes with a whole new set of problems. What are the legal ramifications? Where does the customer stand on stopped work? What are going to do with employees that aren't billable? Make sure your contract addresses this issue.

Spreadsheet Line Items

Because our firm believed in telling the customer more than they may have wanted to know we moved the line items on the estimate spreadsheets directly to the invoice. In doing so the client could, if they wished, cross-reference the invoices directly to the estimate attached to the contract.

Sending it out

Our contracts always had a place for the name, address, and phone number of the person who receive and paid the invoices. The closer we could get to the right desk the better. And when it came time to collect we knew exactly where the invoice was sitting.

Prior to the Due Date

It didn't always work but we tried to make a call a day or two prior to receiving the payment to make sure it went out. Some customers allowed the call and some didn't. We tried not to overstep our bounds. If we couldn't call before and the payment was two days late they got a call whether they agreed with it or not.

Faxing

We heard, on a regular basis, that the invoice was lost or not received. Along with the calls we made, before and after, we always faxed a copy.

[A Story: We once had a customer that was late paying. We called and he said he hadn't receive an invoice and then got mad because we faxed him a duplicate. He said he got it mixed up with the original.]

Collecting

> I realize this is a difficult part of the business for a lot of people but you need to remember that you're in a business that exchanges dollars for services rendered and if you've rendered services and the customer does not want to pay... they still must.
>
> I would suggest the following: Begin the collection process with phone calls, faxes and or letters. You don't want the client to say they just didn't know. If the simple stuff doesn't work send a registered letter. If that doesn't work, move up to a letter from your attorney. If all else fails turn it over to a collection agency. But before you take this last step make sure that your project book, time sheets, and daily notes are all up to date. You've already lost money and you don't want to lose more by finding out you're at fault.

Other Accounting

Deposits

If you've agreed on an upfront deposit make sure that it is invoiced for and collected before you start work.

3rd party products

If the contract stipulates the need for 3rd party products to used in the development, make sure the payments are made up front. You don't want to stop a project or pay for software if you don't have to.

Make sure that if the client pays for the purchase of software, that it's provided to him once the project is complete.

Chapter 14   Revenues and the Contract

Introduction - Revenue

The reason we're in business is to make money, though all too often I watch software development firms act as if they're were not.

I constantly reminded my staff that business is the agreed upon exchange of value. We do something for one hour and in return we will receive one hour's worth of revenue. To do anything else is pro bono and we're not attorneys.

Charging for Services Rendered

It has be understood and drilled home every day, if necessary, that the owner of a business has a responsibility to the business and to themselves and their employee, to optimize the firms ability to accomplish billable work, a service, and to charge for the work that's completed, or rendered.

Methods of Charging for services rendered

There are several ways to charge for developing software. You can charge time and materials, fixed bid, or combination of both, but whichever method is used there are ramifications.

Charging Time and Materials

The best method of charging a client for services rendered is to charge them for each and every hour spent. This method affords you, the provider, with flexibility so that, if you go over in hours because of a misjudgment you'll still get paid for "all" the hours spent. The benefit to the customer is that if the project is done in less than the estimated hours they're not charged for the remaining hours. This type of contract really only protects the provider.

A Fixed Bid

The most uncomfortable way to write a contract, from a development firm's point of view, is to do a fixed bid. This method affords you little room for additional charges if you run over. Though at the same time, if you can get it done in less time you collect the additional margin. This type of contract only protects the customer.

The Lynch Pin

The determining factors as to whether a contract will be successful, time and materials or fixed, are: the quality of the specification, the estimate, and the ability of your developers to carry it off. Three areas that are addressed by people that have families, holidays, vacations, personal problems, good days and bad. This doesn't take into account the language you're using is only in beta, the patches aren't ready yet, and memory in the machines is bad.

With all the parameters out of your control there's still a way to make sure you're covered.

The Contract – A way that works for both Parties

I'd like to suggest that there's a better way to write an agreement. An agreement that, if the project has changes to the original specification, and affects the hours needed to make the adjustments, the provider gets paid for service rendered and at the same time the customer is protected from a constantly open ended and

The Operation and Management of a Software Company

changing contract. An open-ended contract they are often reluctant to sign.

Let me present the basic make up of such an agreement. For lack of a better name lets call it a "closed-ended time and material" contract. The basic points are:

1. Make the contract time and materials. Explain to the customer that you will not charge them for going over in hours, unless there are change orders. If you are under in hours the customer will not be charged for the unused hours.

2. If there are changes to the original specification, at the completion of the project you will bill the contracted price plus the cost of the change orders.

By writing a contract this way;

1. The <u>customer</u> is assured that if hours are not spent they're not charged for them. The customer can review the spreadsheets per this qualification.

2. The <u>customer</u> understands that if any agreed upon changes are made to the original specification and therefore additional hours are necessary they will be charged for those changes. Use of customer sign off on Change Orders will provide validation of agreement.

3. The <u>provider</u> is assured that any additional work, big or small will be paid for. The customer's signature on the Change Orders will provide assurance of agreement.

Tracking Time

With such a tightly written contract it's important that the hours of every staff member be tracked.

The Company Lawyer

"Before you make any adjustments to your contracts make sure you checked with your attorney as to the correctness of each."

Project Manager

With this type of a contract it is even more important that your project manager stay on top of the staff and client.

Note

The contract that follows is one that I have used for many projects. Is it correct? Should it be used? The answer is no. It's just an example. Please consult your attorney and have a contract written by them, specifically for you.

Customer's Business Name
Software Development Services Agreement

Date: 02/12/02

Presented to:

Name, Pres.
Business Name
1234 Euclid Ave.
Cleveland, Ohio 44444

330-123-4567 Office
330-123-4567 Fax

Presented by:

Name, Pres.
Company Name
1234 Euclid Ave.
Cleveland, Ohio 44444

Lminer@abscdef.com
(330) 123-4567 x123 Office
(330) 123-4567 Fax

Your Company's Name
Software Development Services Agreement

Client Name: _____ Date:
02/12/2002

_____
_____
_____

Cost of Services Rendered.:

The hourly rate to be charged under this contract is: $ 00.00

Start Date:

The start date for this contract is: Wed. 02/19/04

Type of Contract:

This contract is to be considered a 'Time and Materials' contract for all software development services rendered with an estimated completion time of 00 hours.

Product to be Delivered:

Software Development Services per client request / direction. Please see pg. 4 - 6 of this document for specific details.

Ownership of Source Code:

All results, per services rendered, under this contract are the sole property of the {Client named above}

Client Support in the Development Process:

The {Client named above} will be consistently available to (Your Company's Name) personnel to answer and or respond to any inquires by designated (Your Company's Name) Corporation personnel.

Contiguous Effort:

Once this contract is made started, a continuing effort by all parties must be put forth. Any 'unreasonable downtime' caused by the {Client named above} which causes (Your Company's Name) development staff downtime, will be reflected in the final delivery date.

Nondisclosure:

This document is to be considered a nondisclosure agreement between {Client named above} and (Your Company's Name). While working for {Client named above}, (Your Company's Name) will not discuss any information, with any parties, on any subject pertaining to the project within this document, or the business practices {Client named above}, without authorized permission of authorized personnel of {Client named above}.

Your Company Name - Employees:

For a period of 24 months from the completion of this Agreement {Client named above} will not approach (Your Company's Name) employee(s), for employment purposes without authorized permission from an authorized party of the (Your Company's Name).

{Client named above}Employees:

For a period of 24 months from the completion of this Agreement (Your Company's Name) will not approach {Client named above} employee(s), for employment purposes without authorized permission from an authorized party of the {Client named above}.

Material Costs:

We don't foresee the need for any additional software being needed, but if authorized by {Client named above} the cost of the additional software is to be covered by {Client named above}

Development Site:

The software development services will be delivered at both {Client named above} business offices and (Your Company's Name) business offices. .

Payment Terms:

Services are invoiced as follows.

1.) (Your Company's Name) will bill {Client named above} once every 2 weeks for services rendered, unless services rendered constitutes less than 40 hours. If service rendered are less than 40 hours {Client named above} will be invoice immediately upon completion of services.

2.) Terms on invoices will be 15 days from date of invoice.

If this Document is satisfactory and all parts of the document are agreed upon, please see below.

{Client named above}

Signed;

_____   _____

Date

    Authorized

    Accounts Payable Contact Name : _____

    Address: _____

    City, State, Zip:_____

    (Your Company's Name)

_____   _____
Name, Pres. -   Company Name   Date

Chapter 15   Other Revenue / Support

Introduction

Even though your firm is focused on software development, there are some other services you may want to address that will complement your software development efforts.

A Web Site

You probably already have one, but if you don't take the time to get one built. And once you do use it to augment every part of your business.

From the sales side make all your literature accessible. Add email for your customers; add email directly to you managers and staff, put up sample applications, and seminars or projects you've completed. Anything you do to reduce paper and enhance your sales dept is to your advantage

Let Project Mangers and developers use it to communicate with the customer. Have secure logins to allow your clients to review their projects.

Let accounting use it to interact with customers. If you can, let your accounting software be accessible to the customers, making it a tool to increase cash flow.

Intranet

If you don't have an Intranet, build one now. Use it to collect automated time sheets. Have your developers build an internal library for code. Put your handbook and insurance information up on it.

E-Commerce

Think about what you do for your customers every day. You build sites that earn income. Well, do it for yourself. Find something that is manageable and build an e-commerce site for yourself. It'll be good experience, show your customers that you can build quality product, and adds to the revenue stream at the same time.

External - Client Extras

There are a few other things you might want to consider to earn extra income. They're not time consuming or difficult.

Site Maintenance

Write a contract for continuing updates of your client's web sites. It saves the customer money, increase your cash flow, and keeps you close to your customer.

Hosting

If you can host sites do it. Again, it will increase your cash flow and keep you closer to your customer. An important aspect of staying close is that once the customer invests in your abilities, there will be a greater likelihood of doing more work for them.

Traffic Monitoring

Monitoring traffic across your customer's web site is a great add-on to the services you already provide. It allows for discussion of what's working and what isn't and also increases the chances of getting more work as the site is adjusted.

Chapter 16   Purchases

Introduction - Purchases

Keeping a software development firms supplied with hardware and software can be costly. Every new developer requires a computer, a connection to the network, more software, and time. The following is just a brief discussion on how to handle some of the costs.

Desk and Chair

Ok, maybe desk and chairs aren't hardware and software but I want to get a plug in here for the developers. If you want to spend some extra cash, this is the place to do it. You may not sit in one place all day long but your staff does. Make them comfortable.

Hardware and peripherals

So now the developer is comfortable and ready to go, how about the machine?

As mentioned in a previous chapter you should have a developers committee. Ask their thoughts on the machines. In fact, let a senior developer shop for the best machines. They know more about what they need than you do and can discuss all the options with a supplier. If you do it you'll just be the middleman in anyway.

I would caution you though, that like anyone else your staff will want the fastest, coolest machine out there, whether they really need it or not. Be aware and discuss the real needs vs. the perceived. If you haven't already, start with the software you're running and work backward to the size of the machine with one or two version ahead taken into account.

Standardize on one manufacturer if you can. It'll be easier to swap parts and build a relationship with one sales person. It can really help out in a pinch. Do the same with NIC cards and peripherals.

If you're a single shift shop then one machine per developer is what you're doing. If you're a multiple shift shop then I would suggest swappable hard drives. Have a librarian check them in and out for safe storage.

The last thing you want to do is waste your time or your employee's time on hardware issues. Get it standardized, keep extra inventory, and be ready to make the swap and get back to work.

Software

Boxed

Let your in-house committee decide on what's purchase. Try to standardize. You're far better off using one type of application that everyone can learn, than three than no one knows.

In-house

Every firm has in-house applications they use. Have the staff that uses it continuously point out improvements and use any down time to make enhancements.

Also consider that if the in-house application works for you it could work for others. Think about boxing it up and selling it.

The Operation and Management of a Software Company

The Clients

When a project is finished inform the customer that you're removing the application from your workstations and servers. The only way you should leave it on your machines and / or in your possession is if the customer has signed a service contract to do so. The reason for this is that the client may perceive an implied willingness on your part to store their software in case they lose or destroy their copies and you have no intention to do so.

[A Story: In the early 90's we did a lot of work for a large accounting firm. The software tracked the company's workflow. In early 2000 they called to ask if we had copies of the software we had written for them. It seems that they never backed up the source code or the executable over those 10 odd years. We couldn't help them.]

Library

If you haven't already, start a code library for your developers. Software developers are famous for reinventing the wheel. Have your development committee decide where it resides and what goes in and then make sure that everyone knows it. Assign a librarian.

Old Hardware

As your machines get older move them to a test room that you can use to test processors and older versions of operating systems that your customers will surely still have.

Old Software

Hang on to it. I can promise you'll have a customer from ten years ago that will call and ask if that FOXPRO DOS application can be modified, just a little bit.

Chapter 17   Building a History

Introduction - Building a History

With all the work that goes into doing a project, externally for the customer and internally for your company it's important that a history of all the events be kept and analyzed. We'll discuss each part of the process and what it tells you.

Design Specifications – As written

If you want a serious critique of your design specifications as it's written, before the developers beat it up, find an outside party that's willing and able. Go over the document from every perspective, from grammar and sentence structure to technical competence.

Remember that the design document is going to be around for several years, inside and out, and it represents the quality of work your firm is capable of. So make sure you get it right.

Design Specification Contracts

Take a look at the design spec contract once the design specification is written and delivered. Was anything left out that you not wish had been put in? From simple things such as drive time to changing the terms?

Make a list of items, no matter how unimportant they may seem, and discuss them with your staff and company attorney.

Project Estimations – Before and After

One of the most important reviews you can do is to compare the initial estimate with the adjusted one at the completion of the project.

1. Determine if the hours for each line item were correctly estimated. This is your company's first set of quality controls. You need to determine, if there were miscalculations, whether they were based on a flaw in the estimating, in the design spec, or the abilities of the developers.

2. Determine if your efficiency rates used to calculate the hours per day are correct. If you calculated your efficiency rate and used it to determine days or weeks and you didn't hit your delivery date your earlier number was incorrect and needs to be adjusted. Understand that every number you get out of the before and after spreadsheets can be used to fine-tune the next project. You need to see this process of analysis as an iterative technique to better estimates.

3. Determine if the delivery dates were meet.

    Was all the delivery dates met? It may take going back to the time sheets to determine this but it's important to know and the spreadsheets will give you the direction to begin an investigation.

4. Determine and document all overruns.

    Overruns are based on the actual billable hours vs. the projected billable hours. Find out who and why and then determine a course of action. Fixing the reason for the overruns now will determine profitability on the next project.

The Operation and Management of a Software Company

With the help of accounting, determine the margins made on the project.

You don't always know what your real margins are on a project until you've wrapped it up. Use your accounting department to run through all the numbers and give you a real % margin on the project. If you find that you made less than you expected go back and find out why and correct the process that led to the loss.

Design Specifications – As used by the developers

Take a look at the physical design spec once the developers have finished using them. Ask them to turn them in. Review their hand written notes to see, if you can determine, with the developers help, what needs changed to make the next project easier.

Change Orders

Collect the change orders out of the project book and categorize them. Did the customer or the project manager, or the developer make the changes? Were they unforeseen, or did the project itself change?

Make a list and work with the staff to make sure, if your company dropped the ball, then the items are addresses in the next specification and specification template.

Issue Orders

The same goes for Issue Orders. Collect and categorize them. Were the issues customer oriented or your firm's doing?

Again, make a list and work with the staff, project manager through developers, to make sure that they don't arise again.

Employee Time Sheets

This is an important analysis. Collect the employee's time sheets and analyze the efficiency rate of each, during a specific project. First, did they meet expectations? If not, can you isolate an area that caused the drop?

It's important to correlate the timesheets and the project. It will allow you an awareness of your staff's real capabilities.

Billing / Invoicing Information

It's always advantageous to review billable and payment schedules once the project is finished. I'd suggest that you ask a qualified bookkeeper or accountant to do it with you. Three ideas that can help are:

1. Decide whether you want this company as a customer again.

2. Decide whether you need to increase or decrease hourly rate on the next project.

3. Decide whether you should change the payment terms.

Chapter 18 Business Plan

Introduction

The first thing you need to know about the Business Plan is that no one really enjoys writing it let alone taking time out of the day to even think about it.

I'm not going to add an outline because there are plenty of books on the subject.

Now even though it is an unpleasant task, you really do need to sit down and begin putting a plan together. I'll explain the reasons but if you don't have time to write a formal plan just begin to make notes on a separate pad of paper. Carry it around with you. Begin with the easy things in your company. The things you know. Write down where you've been and where you are now. Quantify where you are. How many months you've been in business? How many employees, clients, and projects do you have? Just start expanding on what you've written. Go from where you are to where you want to be. Understand this plan doesn't ever have to be typed up or formalized. It's your business and you're plan.

The real reason every owner, manager, president, general manager needs to write a business plan? Because in the process of collecting all of the information in one place, onto one pad of paper, you reflect on where you've been and where you want to go. The writing of a plan, whether it's the business plan or the to-do's for next week is an exercise in planning how to get from where you are to where you want to go.

An alternative is to start with where you want to go instead of where you've been. Write down what your company is going to look like in year one, in two, and in three. How many employees and how large offices are you going to need? What's it going to cost you? Then take the year three numbers and calculate backwards as to just how you're going to get there. How many salespeople are you going to need, where do you need to locate your office? When these details are laid out on that yellow legal pad you've got plan. You've always wanted a roadmap, some questions answers, and some advice. Now take your own. Follow the direction we've just written down.

[A Comment: When I started I didn't want to bother with a business plan but at some point, after the first couple of years, I did pick up a couple books and start writing. What I found was that is was exciting to write down where I had been and what I had accomplished. But even more exciting was writing down where I wanted to go. And every year after that I made a effort to beat the plan I had written the previous year and I did. I didn't go nuts with my projections; I just wanted to add five developers or have five more good customers or wanted our first Internet project.]

Think about your business plan as a roadmap that you'll take a little bit of time to write, say a week or two, on and off, in the car, at the end of the day, and use it to follow the rest of the year. It is a lot easier to do this way than spending every day of the coming year trying to figure out where to go next. You'll already know.

An example of a business plans follows

The Operation and Management of a Software Company

Example #1 - Table of Contents – Business Plan

Section 1.0

    Business Purpose

    Executive Summary

        Our Services
        Our Product
        Distinguishing Features of Company Name Inc.
        Attractiveness to the Market
        Risk Factors
        Structure
        Summary of Financial Projections

Section 2.0

    Projected Financial Statements

Section 3.0

        Management Team
        About Owner / Senior Management
        About Sales Force
        Key Outside Advisors
        Company Name Inc. Services
        Company Name Inc. Products
        The Market
        Market Strategy
        Advertising Strategy
        The Competition
        The Business Facility

Section 4.0

Marketing Plan

Section 5.0

Sales Plan

Example #2 - Table of Contents – Business Plan

Cover Page

Table of Contents

Company Name, Inc. Mission Statement

Company Name, Inc. Philosophy

Executive Summary

The Company

    Company Strategy

        History
        Current Status
        Future Prospects

    Management Team

        Training
        Support
        Incentives

    Project Management Team

        Training
        Support
        Incentives

    Development Team

        Training
        Support
        Incentives

Marketing Team

    Training
    Support
    Incentives

Sales Team

Corporate Facilities

Use

Hardware

Software

Layout

The Market –

    Customer benefits
    What is the market?
    The competition

The Products / Services

    Product / Service Features
    Pricing
    Production

    Warranties / Repair

Sales and Promotion –

Selling Guidelines

    Executive Selling
    In-House Sales Force

        Training
        Support
        Incentives

    Sales Representatives

    Promotions

    Finances

2004 Details

Next Year Projections

Chapter 19 Customer Service

Introduction

I have to tell you from my experiences that a large majority of software development houses have a long way to go in providing good service to their customers. Why that is I'm not sure. Whether it's because we're just a bunch of developers that would really rather code or we know better than the customer, or we just never learned what customer services means.

Years ago I worked for the research facility of a large tire company. Once you were there for a while you were informed that you had one of two career ladders to climb. You could select either management or scientific. On the scientific one you were trained or could opt to go back school. On the management track you were left to you own devices. There was no management training.

This kind of thing happens far to often in software development firms. You've been on the computer science track for a long time and now its time to start a business, which is a management position, for which you've not been trained or are prepared.

Start at the beginning

Customers that come to you want the same thing they want when they shop for a car, they want quality service. They want someone that will explain things, show them all the options, be honest and up front, and let them know what they can expect. It's the same when selling development services.

Sales Visits

Build an honest up front relationship with your customer. When the sales call is complete make sure that you follow up on everything you said you would do, immediately.

Meetings

Come on ... pay attention to your customer. Stop showing them how smart you are and listen to what they have to say. I've been in so many meetings that the technical people talk so far over the customer's head that it's embarrassing. When you talk, talk to the level of person across from you. He or she can't be impressed by words they don't understand.

And be prepared. Try to anticipate what the customer wants to talk about and have the information at hand. Have more than they want to talk about if you can. Too often I hear that we don't have to prepare. It's just a "get to know you" meeting. Look, it's better to have way too much than not enough. Have an agenda ready. You don't have to use it but it's easier if you lead the discussion and follow up on all details after the meeting.

Design Specification

Make sure that your customers feel they're participating in the design of their software. Make the process of writing this document a joint effort.

During the writing process I'll pass the customer a chapter allowing them to participate in its development. Sometime they read it and sometimes they don't but it's important that they are vested in the project.

If you do, the final product will be much better and the customer will have as much ownership and pride as you do.

Contracts

Before the specification is completed show the customer an example of your development contract. Begin to have discussion on all the paragraphs. The customer will find it a lot easier to sign that way.

Developing the Application

Keep the customer completely informed during the development process. Some suggestions are:

1. Set reporting milestones

2. Continually show the customer the software being developed.

3. Make the spreadsheets, with billable hours accounted for, available to the customer.

4. Ask the customer for a sign off on each screen, report, table, milestone, etc.

5. Give out your email address as well as the developers'.

6. Give out your phone number, office, cell and fax, as well as the developers'.

7. Place the software up on a web site where it can be view and or tested.

8. Invite the customer in to your office for periodic reviews.

Realize that the more informed your customer is, the easier it'll be on you and the project manager.

Remember that customer service is about building a reputation.

Product Delivery

The first thing to do when delivering the product is to make sure that there is a warranty in place. With a warranty your customer knows exactly where to turn the minute the applications starts in production.

Some other things you may want to consider.

1. Have a wrap up session with the customer.

2. Have a separate wrap up session with your staff. Go over any of the analysis with them.

3. Have an internal document review / analysis soon after the project is completed.

4. Deliver bound manuals and a copy of the Project Book.

5. Deliver extra copies of the application on CD with any documentation included.

6. A thank you note

Follow Up

Stay on top of "your" work. The client may have paid for it but it's still your reputation. Call or visit the customer and users of the application. Even when the warranty expires keep making calls. Stay close to your customers for both service and business reasons.

More

Customer Service doesn't mean just during the project. Other things we might suggest;

1. Make sure your invite them to seminars and open houses.

2. Keep the client up to date on the languages, databases, patches, upgrades, and service packs used in the their application.

3. Let the customer know about seminars that would be of interest to them, even though you may not host them.

4. Keep them up to date on virus and bug fixes.

Chapter 20   Marketing and Sales

Introduction

This chapter is about the external part of your business, finding and capturing customers. It's not so much a how to; there are a lot of books on sales and marketing. It is more a perspective of what I discovered as I built my company.

First and foremost I think you need to understand what type of business you're in and it isn't correct to say software. Yes, you may write software but the real business you're in is service. You're one of many services to your customers. You need to know that your customers have a lot of other vendors and you'll be judged on the quality of services rendered, not on the way you write SQL queries.

If you think your exceptional skill, at developing software, is going to have them pounding down the door you should consider another line of work. There are a lot of brilliant developers out there and if you can't serve your customer the way they want to be served, you're going to be out of business real fast.

What brings in customers is getting your organization noticed, and getting noticed is called marketing. The concept of marketing to a computer science guy is like asking your George W. Bush to talk in complete sentences. It just isn't going to happen without a lot of effort.

Marketing

A Definition

mar·ket·ing (*noun*)

1. **The selling of products or services:** the business activity of presenting products or services to potential customers in such a way as to make them eager to buy. Marketing includes such matters as the pricing and packaging of the product and the creation of demand by advertising and sales campaigns.

Presenting Products and Services – Physically

Presenting what we do is difficult. We write software applications that belong to other people, to corporations, so you can't or shouldn't just pull out the latest one you've written to show, at least not without permission. So for all intents and purposes you're selling a set of services that the customer can't see or touch until they pay for a design specification and several months' development. Sound right?

Here's what I would suggest:

First, get permission to show the applications you've written. Your customer may be somewhat reluctant but let them know you can take off their name or agree to only show it to potential customers outside their industry.

Second, take a hint from advertising agencies, make screen prints of the applications and place them in a portfolio. Not necessarily all the screens but the important one. Build a story of each application and the screens you've selected.

Third, when you get permission, get a letter from the client addressing the quality of your services. Add it to the portfolio.

Fourth, if you can build a automated presentation, do it. Start with a power point presentation on your laptop and move up in sophistication, as you're able.

One thing we have to get over in this industry is the false notion that our skills will have them pounding down the door. We need to remember that our customers need be sold and selling takes marketing. Think about it this way: if they can't find the door they can't walk through it.

Presenting Your Product as a Service

I realize I keep repeating myself but what you're selling is a service.

Think about your own process when selecting a service. What makes you call the furnace guy and say, "You got the job". I believe you selected the winner on how he treated you, the attention he gave and the speed of responding. I would bet that you didn't ask for references and you didn't visit other customer's basements. You selected the guy on his presentation and that's exactly how your customers are going to select you.

Now, you should be prepared with references, testimonials and employee résumé, because they are important. But I have found that the majority of your customers, right or wrong, are going to select you on your presentation and everything it communicates.

News Releases

The word on press releases is to use them as often as you can. It is the only way you are ever going to get in front of the business community and not pay for the privilege.

Advertising, Marketing, and Communication Agencies

If you don't have experience in one of these three areas then I would suggest that you hire one. You can't go wrong in getting professional support in getting the word out about you business.

Print Advertising

Getting the word out through magazines is complicated if your clients aren't in a very specific vertical market. Advertising in a magazine to attract a even a slim segment of their readership is very expensive and not very efficient. I've always believed you're better off doing a more targeted type of marketing.

Marketing Campaigns

I've tried a lot of things to get my customers' attention, from big seminars to newspaper and magazine ads but only one method really seems to work well and that's targeted direct mail. Why did it work? Because I could select the specific list I wanted to target, with the names and titles, and then tailor the message to their needs. It was one on one instead of one message and a million subscribers. 98% of which weren't interested in what I had to sell.

Mailing Lists

My firm had no specific vertical market. We developed custom software for any firm that needed it. The question we always asked was: if our work is coming from a lot of different vertical markets, from a lot of different directions, how do we better target customers?

The Operation and Management of a Software Company   187

[A Comment: In retrospect I think we should have chased verticals at the same time we were working horizontally.]

The answer was, at least initially, that we targeted those that were using the languages that we were developing in. We located lists that could provide us with people that programmed FoxPro, VB, or C. We then only pulled out the records that had company names. This gave us someone to call

Our message was directed right at the company, its' employees, and their use of the development language. We explained our levels of expertise and offered our support.

We mailed in concentric circles out from our office. We adjusted the message as responses came in making sure that what worked was repeated.

Tailoring the message

The message is everything. Think long and hard about whom's going to read it and what they are going to do with it once they've finished.

The most important thing you can do is put yourself in their place. If they're IT managers, then define their needs, not only on managing hardware and software, but on personal terms. If you send a mailing to developers get their attention and make them want call you or visit your web site? If you can't get into his or her heads then find someone who can. Don't assume you know. It'll cost you a lot of more money for just a few extra hours of work.

[A Story: Here's a real success story in direct mail.

In the summer of 1999 we had our share of web development but found we still weren't getting the amount we wanted. The reason was that a significant majority of web site design and development was going to advertising agencies. It made sense because Agencies were already doing the copy, artwork, and design so why wouldn't they do the web sites. Just because we were experts in the field of software development didn't mean we were going to get the work. They were turning to services organizations they were comfortable with.

So a lot of work around us was heading in the wrong direction. How do we get a piece of the action? We started by reviewing how agencies worked, their skills, and areas of expertise.

In the fall of 1999 we decide that agencies were great at the services they rendered but were struggling to actually do the Internet / database work they were being asked to do. We found that the traditional agency wasn't built to handle a staff of software developer.

So in the fall of 1999 we offered ad agencies a way to continue taking advantage of the Internet boom and be able to undertake every opportunity that came their way. We did it by offering all of our design and development expertise to agencies as away for them to extend their book of services. Their clients didn't need to know they were subcontracting out the work and they could take on all the work that came their way.

This campaign was one for the textbooks. We hit a nerve. We had so many calls we were concerned we couldn't follow up. We did and the result were enormous.]

The Operation and Management of a Software Company

What were the lessons we learned from this?

Do the research up front. Even if it takes longer and costs more, it's worth it.

Find the right list first and for the right cost second. A little legwork will make a big difference.

Work on the message. Take your research and write a message that you believe they'll respond to. Putting a letter in the customer's hand at the wrong time with the wrong message is just a waste of money.

Follow up. Whether you get one call or 200 calls the customer back and call back within minutes. Remember customer service. You didn't go to all this expense to lose the guy because you're to busy. If you're too busy to call them you're certainly too busy to do the work.

You're in the Door

The First Sales Call

As much as I didn't want to believe the old adage about first impressions, it's true. The first meeting is your opportunity to set the impression, the direction, and determine whether you'll be invited back.

What's important is to be prepared. Bring absolutely everything you might want or need to present and make sure that before you leave you set an agenda for the next meeting.

When you leave the meeting make sure that you review it with others in your firm, critiquing what you think went right or wrong. Just doing it in the car on the way back to the office will help.

When you get back to office, do what you said you would do. Send back the information, the references, and the example. Do it the minute you walk in the office.

More Meetings

Ok, the best scenario is that there are no more meetings. You've explained everything to the nth degree. The customer understood absolutely everything. You were wonderful. If they had had their checkbook with them they would have already written you a check!

But really... The fewer meetings you have the better. Meetings are very expensive. We had a rule that every customer got two meetings, no questions asked, at their location, but if they needed a third we always tried to get the customer to come to us. We went as far as to losing customers because we just could not afford to continually go to meetings.

To begin getting control of meetings, document the hours you and others spend in them. Put a dollar value to them and determine if your business can afford to sit around and talk all day.

Explaining the Steps

A good number of your clients do not understand the software development process and so you'll need to explain it to them at one level or another.

I'd suggest you present this information using a document that lays out your development process and do it at the very first meeting. It should take them through the all the steps, from the meetings and contracts to the installation and delivery of the product.

The First Contract

The Specification Contract

Generally the first contract you'll need signed is the contract that allows you to do a design specification. This is the most important psychological barrier you need to get the customer over.

Automating the contract

I'd suggest that you automate your contracts with the specification contract being the first. We've always used Microsoft Word to build contract templates.

Getting it Signed

As I said earlier the first contract is always the toughest. Here's how I explain the specification contract.

"This result of this contract will be your property. The design specification belongs to your firm. It's your intellectual property and not ours. When we create the document we're going to do it together. There'll be sign off's. If there's something we missed it's fixed right away. When the document is complete and signed it's a living document. If you wish you can take this document to any other development firm and get an estimate. It's yours to do with as you wish."

The Second Contract

The development contract is much more specific in lying out all the parameters with which you and the customer will act as the software is being developed.

Following are some of the contract paragraphs I suggest be considered. The basics are:

The Cost

Present the total cost and the number of hours to complete the job.

The Type of Contract

Is this contract a time and materials, fixed bid, or some combination? Spell it out clearly.

Retainer

Is there an upfront retainer? This should be considered if you are concerned about the customer ability to pay.

Additional Costs - 3rd party

These are charges that are separate from the hourly work. It should be understood that once the application is delivered so is the boxed software. They bought it... it's theirs.

The Terms

This is quite simple. Just make sure you present the terms so that the client knows exactly when you're billing them, when they're to pay, and what they can expect payment stopped.

Product to be delivered

You can either lay out, line by line, what you are going to provide the client or, as I would suggest, make the design specification and estimate attachments to the contract.

Start Date/Delivery Date

Provide a start date and an estimate stop or delivery date. Make sure you've taken into account holidays, vacations, and efficiency rates.

Customer Support

Make a point to add client responsibilities to the contract. They'll need to be as available as your developers are. You can quickly eat up billable hours if the customer is not around to answer questions.

No Stopping

This paragraph is important. You do not want to allow the client to stop or slow down in the middle of a project, leaving your developers non-billable.

The reasons for stopping or temporarily halting can be from a vacation to money problems but you need to understand they aren't your firm's problem. If the client slows down, for any reason, you're the one that's going to lose money.

Nondisclosure - No compete

It's only the best way to do business.

Employees – yours and theirs

Simple, you don't take theirs and they don't take yours. Spell it out up front and avoid losing a customer.

Warranty

Everyone makes programming mistakes and as hard as you and your customers try, something is going to get past you. I'd suggest providing a 30-day warranty that says that if they find a "coding error" you will fix it for free. This eliminates a customer who takes delivery, doesn't use the application for months and then says it doesn't work or your developers are on another project and you find yourself without a way to support them.

Getting it Signed

Ok, the specification contract was a psychological hurdle but this contract isn't going to be any easier. You need to understand that you are selling the building of a product that has never existed and when it's complete it's going to sit on a serve somewhere. At least when you build a house you can see it going up, you know there's value in the work being done. In software development you don't necessarily have that. It's tough work but here's where patience comes in.

Automating the Contract

As with the Specification Contract you need to automate the development contract. A template with your standard paragraphs can keep from missing anything

Getting the Work Started

I have to tell you, there is almost nothing like the feeling when a customer signs that contract and pushes it across the table. Then when you come to your senses, shake hands, say thank you, and head for the door ...you hear a little voice behind you saying, "Done yet?"

Chapter 21 Sales vs. Development

Finding a Balance

In all the years that I've done development estimating and contract writing I have always found that there is a tug of war between the estimated hours the developers calculate and the number of hours or the cost the sales department needs to present the customer.

The two lines of thought go something like this.

From the developer's point of view hours are hours; you can't make them shorter. You can't make hours disappear because you still have to do the work, whether they're on paper or not. So, go ahead, cut the hours, it's still going to take the hours estimated and we're going to lose money on another project!

From the sales departments' point of view: Hey, the customer has only so much money and I know what it is and this estimate is too high and I know the other firm estimating this project is going to come in lower and we need the work so if you don't get our numbers down, we'll lose this job and it's your fault.

Prevention

Before you get to this point there are some things that may prevent these discussions from occurring.

1. The sales department needs to present the parameters, hours and cost right up front. All parties should know the numbers and any other parameter before the specification is even written.

2. As the specification is being written there may need to be intermediate estimates made internally to allow the technical writers to adjust their tack with the customer.

3. The technical writer can break down the specification into more distinct pieces allow the sales department to present different phases of development.

4. If a specific cost is predetermined the technical writer / project manager must discuss going back to the customer prior to completion of the specification.

A Resolution

I have taken several tracks in resolving the dilemma presented and naturally I don't want to lose the job any more than anyone else does.

Back to Work – Developers

If the customers' funds are very exact and there is no going over then I ask the development team to go back and see if they can find alternatives, such as 3rd party products, that will allow us to deliver the same product using less hours and cost.

Divide and Conquer – Technical Writer

If the funds are not predetermined but the sales department wants to be cautious I ask the technical writer and developers to divide the project down further into additional phases that the customer can digest.

Visit - Sales

If the funds are not predetermined but the sales department is concerned that at this cost we will lose the job I ask the sales department to go back to the customer and have a frank discussion, explaining that, as designed with their participation, we are concerned that the cost is prohibitive and that we are working hard to make the specification and estimate functional for them.

The Final Decision

If all else fails, we can't get the hours down, we can't break it into any smaller pieces without losing functionality and the customer says they don't want to hear any excuse it's time to make one of three choices;

Drop Your Margin

You know what your margins are. Can you afford to drop them without taking a loss? If you can do it, but only if there isn't another job on the schedule, that pays the standard margin.

We've told our customers that because we were willing to cut the cost we would have to move it further back on our schedule.

Fight

Here's where you're salesman earns his keep. If all the numbers come out right and there isn't a predetermined cost, then the sales person had better get in there and fight for the business.

It's better to have fought for the business and lost than to not have even made the effort.

Understand that the customer has gone this far with you; they have a psychological stake in seeing that the process continues, that the application is developed. It is a difficult sale but it can be made.

Give it Up

Some projects just are not worth taking on. It's ok to turn down a project if the hours are right and the customers can't afford it. It isn't mandated that just because you wrote the spec you have to do the job at a loss. Let it go.

Chapter 22 Document Responsibility

The Documents

The Project Book

Every document that's created in your company, which pertains to a customer, needs to go into a Project Book. Even thought this book needs to be accessible to everyone, the project manager assigned to the project should maintain this book. In doing so, the authenticity of the process will be assured.

At the very least every document below should be placed in the Project Book. The only limited exceptions are the contracts. I would suggest that copies be placed in the book and the originals stored in the accounting department.

1st Meeting Notes

The first meeting notes are naturally the responsibility of the sales person. These notes are important because they will give your staff an idea of the research that needs to be done to satisfy the customer.

Continuing Meeting Notes

These notes will come from both the sales person and the project manager if attending the meetings. If a developer is present, their notes should be included

Understand that you are building a platform from which to sell the customer your services. The more precise the notes everyone takes, the more precise your presentation back to the customer will be.

Specification Writing Contract

The sales department should write the spec contract because they are the direct connect to the customer at this point in time.

Support in writing the contract should come from all the other parties that participated in the previous customer discussions.

Specification Writing Notes

The technical writer will create a set of notes from the interview process with the customer. Even though they will be translated into a design specification they should be kept for future reference.

Specification

The design specification is a product of the technical writer with the support of the development staff.

Estimate

A quality estimate can really only be created by an experienced software developer. There is really no support any other parties can bring to the process of estimating.

Application Development Contract

Again, once the specification is competed and signed off and the estimate is done the sales person should write the development contract.

I would suggest that prior to writing an application development contract all participants meet to discuss the final contract, in detail.

Change Order

The project manager may initially write the Change Order but the final change order should come from the developer with estimated hours attached.

Issue Order

The project manager should write the Issues Order with resolution support from the developers.

Developers Notes

These are distinct developer notes created during the development project.

Developer's Specification

This is the specification document used by the developers during the application software development.

Application Signoffs

The project manager has the responsibility of getting the customer to sign off on all agreed upon milestones, testing, etc.

Notifying the sales department is important in the relationship building areas. If it is time for sign off's the sales department should use this process to their advantage.

Maintenance Contract

As the project nears its' end the sales departments needs to be aware of any and all maintenance contracts that can be written for this particular customer.

Invoices

The only department that should address AP/AR is accounting. If payment is delinquent the sales department and project manager should be notified.

Note

The following chart presents the responsibilities in chart format.

Document Creation

	Accounting Department	Sales Department	Project Management	Technical Writer	Development Staff
		○			
Next Meetings		○			
Spec Writing Contract		○			
Spec Writing Notes				○	
Specification				○	
Estimate					○
Application Contract		○			
Change Orders					○
Issue Orders					○
Developer Notes					○
Developer's Specification					○
Application Signoff			○		
Maintenance Contract		○			
Invoices	○				
Project Book			○		

Chapter 22: Document Responsibility

Document Support

	Accounting Department	Sales Department	Project Management	Technical Writer	Development Staff
1st Meeting		●			
Next Meetings		●	○		
Spec Writing Contract		●	○	○	○
Spec Writing Notes				●	
Specification				●	
Estimate			○	○	●
Application Contract		●	○	○	○
Change Orders			○		●
Issue Orders			○		●
Developer Notes					●
Developer's Specification					●
Application Signoff		○	●		○
Maintenance Contract		●	○		
Invoices	●	○			
Project Book			●		

Chapter 23 Optimizing Jobs for Efficiency

Introduction

This chapter is a discussion of the number of jobs you take, the length of each job and optimizing your staff for full efficiency.

A Challenge

Every time I spoke to my sales staff I challenged them to drown the development side of the business in work. I actually bet them they couldn't do it. They never did.

The Number of Jobs

Managing the jobs that come into a development business is a lot like being the production control manager in a steel plant. You have to make sure you have the equipment, the manpower and the time to accomplish what's being asked of you. Then you can say yes, we can do that.

Though there are many sophisticated ways of getting production under control, the fastest way is to set up a chart, using Microsoft Excel. Plot the weeks across the bottom, for the whole year, using a week ending date, plot everyday, and the employee's names up the left side. As the jobs come in and the staff is assigned, shade in the squares. Shade out every square to the end date of the project. This simple process will show you where the holes are in your billable hours.

What I would suggest is to shade the holes, the days or weeks with no contract work, with red and then hand them to you sales staff. They'll get the picture... no pun intended.

One thing that's going to get in the way of this perfect scenario is that just about every client wants his or her work done immediately. With this scenario you're chart will be very short in length and very tall in staff.

So which way do you go? More work faster or less work longer? I promise you, it's a question that's asked just about every day.

Here's what I would suggest. Take a look at what you can handle at one time and consider whether the customer will find someone to do it sooner.

If you can handle more work, you can handle the cash flow issues, and the client will walk if you don't ... take the job.

So how do you find more developers fast? The best way is to have start looking months ago into two areas, subcontractors and offshore developers. The best thing to do is to make friends with both these services and make sure they can supply you with staff for more immediate needs. And do it before this situation happens.

If you can't handle more work and / or decide cash flow won't handle it then you have two viable options, and these you should have been prepared for. The first is to negotiate to have the customer wait and more often than not this is through reducing your rate. How low can you go to see this job stays on your calendar? The second less obvious option is to subcontract the job out to another company. This will leave your workforce at present levels, done correctly not interfere with cash flow, and allow you to keep the customer.

The Length of Each Jobs

The best jobs you can take are those that are longer in terms of weeks. What's long? I would suggest that 3 months or 12 week is the beginning of smoothing out your workforce in terms of efficiency and efforts.

What I mean by this is that the more short jobs you have the more stop and go you have and the more non-billable hours you carry. If short jobs were necessary to take then I would schedule them in between the stop of one larger job and the beginning of the other.

Optimizing for Efficiency

The reality is larger jobs allow your staff to increase efficiency rates. As has been said with the larger project the stop and go is decreased but also there begins to be a rhythm to the job. I'm not saying I know exactly what it is but when everything is going along smoothly and everyone has a job to do the rates will go up.

The Bottom Line

So the bottom line is that larger, longer projects will make you more revenue just based on the efficiency rate, let alone the length. At the same time you will have to take smaller projects and they will cut into your revenue stream but the more careful you are the less harm they will do.

Note

The following chart presents the need to locate and manage long term projects.

Chapter 23: Optimizing Jobs for Efficiency

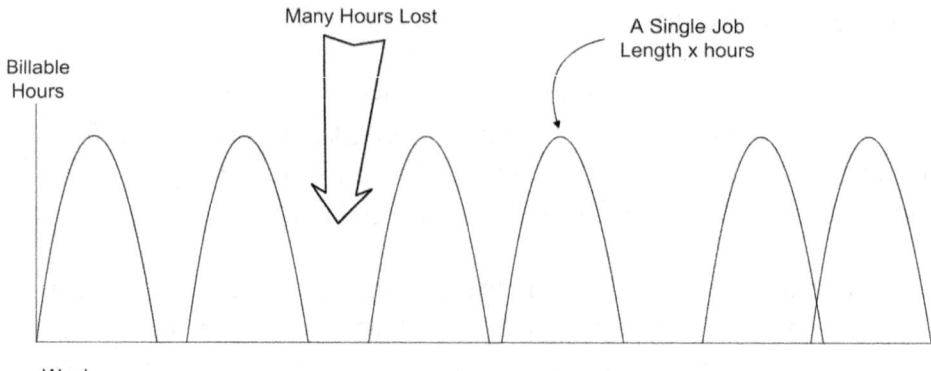

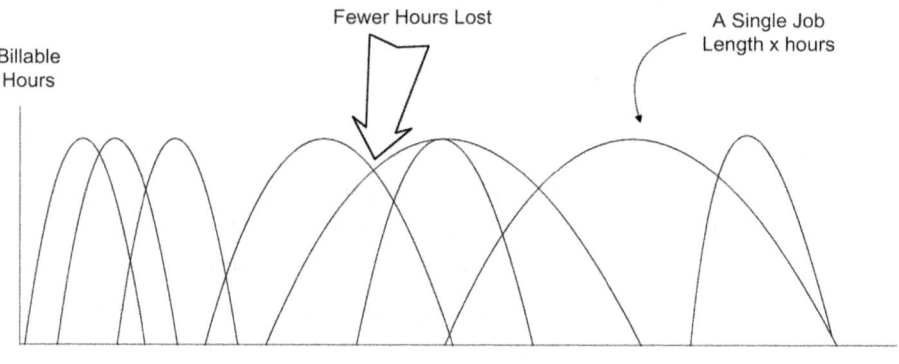

Chapter 24 Earning a Living Wage

In the last twenty years I've had the wonderful opportunity to meet and discuss the software development business with a wide range of entrepreneurs, each unique and hard working in their drive to start, build and grow their firms.

But there seems to be one recurring practice that disturbs me when I discuss how much money they take out of the business. All too often the answer is "little if any".

The answers to why "so little" were wide ranging, from wanting to reinvest in the company to they're just not making enough to pay themselves a wage. They might take out enough to pay the bills at home, to breakeven so to speak, but they aren't taking out a wage that allows them any comfort.

Now I'm not saying that this practice is right or wrong but I want to make a point, from practical experience, if you're one of these people.

The work you do is very hard, the hours very long, and the risks are high. You "must" earn a living wage. Though it's sometimes a necessity to reinvest or go without a paycheck on occasion, don't get caught doing it all the time. It can become a vicious cycle that delivers so little in the end. If your salary is the difference between success and failure you should reconsider your position.

[A Comment. I have to say that I was one of those people I spoke of above. The first year I'm not sure I took anything out. In years two through four, I took out enough to pay the bills and year five through fifteen I earned a fair wage, not an enormous amount, but I was comfortable.

Now, looking back across those fifteen years of hard work I should have taken more out. I should have, at some point, started looking out for myself as much as I looked out for the company.]

Chapter 25 Managing Stress

Stress on the Developers

The stress on the developers whether self imposed or placed there by other staff members, is enormous. Consider what it's like to sit in one place all day, staring at a monitor, writing code line by line day after day.

A lot of what has been written in this book is meant to relieve that stress, from allowing flex hours to supplying lunches, to giving the staff a voice through committees. Anything you can do as a manager to take the weight of every day duties off their shoulders will provide them with a less stressful environment.

[A story; I always noticed the stress, especially when deadlines loomed near. I had seen what it could do to some very good young people when they weren't prepared for it.

In the summer of 2000 my wife suggested that she give yoga classes to the staff. She explained that she could design a class that allowed the developers to relax while setting for long hours. We gave it a try. For an hour a week she taught stretching and relaxation methods to a group of software developers that were used to rocking back and forth in their chairs for 8 hours.

Though the classes were met with some skepticism the first week, we found that the staff began to use what they learned. You could see them stretching and relaxing, in their chairs, at their desks, as the weeks went on. We were eventually asked to purchase a yoga book that could be passed around the office. It was gladly provided.]

Stress on the Owner

It may be a hard thing to understand right now but you're going to pay for it in the end if you don't get a handle on the stress that develops from working all the time. I know far too many owners that make their business their lives. They go to work at 6am and leave at midnight, seven days a week. They don't see their wives or the kids and generally turn into basket cases a few months.

The main reasons for putting in all this time seems to be for one of two reasons. Either they think the business can't run without them or as I've said in the previous chapter they're running to just keep up.

If you think the business can't run without you, you're dead wrong. The people you've hired can do the job if you'll just allow them. Learn to delegate the workload. As we talked about in previous chapters, figure out what you do best and do that, not everyone else's job.

And if you're running to just keep up then maybe you need more employees, more business, or more support. Take a little time out for yourself. Raise your head and take a look around. Try to find out why you're running at full tilt while a lot of others aren't.

I'll finish by saying that even though we all have our egos, our self worth, and sometimes a lot of money tied up in our businesses; none of it is worth a damn if you've lost your family or friends, laid up in the hospital or dead. Take some time to enjoy the rewards of all the hard work.

[A Comment; speaking from experience; I was one of those that ended up in the hospital a couple times because of stress. I'm telling you right now. The stress isn't worth it. Your health isn't worth it. Find a way to manage it and you'll be around to enjoy the fruits of your efforts.]

Chapter 26 Risk

Building and managing a software development business is a risk, a risk that thousands take each year and every year some survive, but the majorities does not. What's the difference between them?

From experience I can tell you that the ones that survive aren't the ones that work an enormous number of hours every day. Brut force in this business just doesn't work any more. But the cliché of "working smart not hard" truly does apply.

The ones that survive are the ones that strive, every day, to get everything right. They're the ones that understand that the fundamentals of accounting, marketing, management and sales will put them ahead of so many of their competitors.

Successful businesses work everyday to do everything right and thereby lowering the risk that they will fail. Its hard work, no denying it, but it's worth every minute.

Chapter 27 Partners

A discussion of partners is as difficult to write about, as they are to have.

What I would say first and foremost about partners is that you need to spend as much time picking one, as you expect them to be around.

The reason for this is that what you now think is a good partnership will come down to personalities, more than it ever will to skills, knowledge and access.

Set expectations early, document everything and work hard on a contractual agreement that allows you as much control or flexibility as you'll need to continue growing your business.

Good partnerships are rare. They are few differences between a marriage and a partnership except in growing a business you're going to spend more time with your partner.

Chapter 28 About the Author

Since 1972 Mr. Miner has worked in the field of technology. Beginning with the U.S. Navy and its sonar and missile control systems he has made the world of technology and computer science his area of expertise.

Receiving advance training in electronics, a degree in computer science, and further training in engineering and artificial intelligence Mr. Miner has made the business of design, development and delivery of software his career.

In the early 1980's he developed 360 degree modeling capabilities for Finite Element Analysis for a leading research facility. In the mid 1980's it was onto artificial intelligence for the power industry and steel industry.

Mr. Miner is nothing if not an entrepreneur. In 1985 he created his first boutique software engineering firm that would become a leader in the custom software design and development. With the successful sale of his organization in 2000, he turned his sites to both building other technology firms and writing a book that will become the center of support for the business of software development entrepreneurs in the U.S.

Mr. Miner was Founder and President of S.E.A. Group, Inc. as well as the same for Branded Browsers and ContinuousPlay Inc. He has also acted as the CEO/COO of Digital Power, President of TRIA Group, Inc. and is now writing a second book on the Software Development Life Cycle (SDLC).

Mr. Miner continues today to focus on the both technology and the business of software design, development and delivery.

For more information contact:

Larry Miner
PO Box 587
Bath, Ohio 44210

Email: larry.miner@gmail.com

www.ingramcontent.com/pod-product-compliance
Lightning Source LLC
Chambersburg PA
CBHW071415170526
45165CB00001B/279